£20

D1356864

THE KINGDOM
OF SAUDI ARABIA

The Kingdom of Saudi Arabia

(Ten successive editions of a work under this title were published by Stacey International between 1977 and 2002. This comprehesively re-created version of *The Kingdom of Saudi Arabia* draws upon the earlier work in its coverage of History and Islam.)

Published by

Stacey International
128 Kensington Church Street
London W8 4BH
Tel: +44 (0)207 221 7166
Fax: +44 (0)207 792 9288
E-mail: marketing@stacey-international.co.uk
Website: www.stacey-international.co.uk

and

Al-Turath
PO Box 68200
Riyadh 11527
E-mail: al-turath@al.turath.com
Website: www.al-turath.com

© 2006 Stacey International

Editor-in-Chief: Max Scott
Design: Graham Edwards

ISBN: 0 9552 1930 2
      9780955219306

Catalogue-in-Publication Data: A catalogue record for this title is available from the British Library

All rights reserved. No part of this publication may be reproduced, stored in a retrieval system, or transmitted in any form or by any means, electronic, mechnical, photographic or otherwise, without prior permission of the copyright owner.

Printing and binding: Oriental Press, Dubai

*Shimmering in the heat haze, the Kingdom Tower (**foreground**) is equalled in height only by the Faisaliyya Tower (**background**), as it towers over the Riyadh's Olayah district.*

THE KINGDOM
OF SAUDI ARABIA

AL-TURATH / STACEY INTERNATIONAL

Principal Contributors to the present version

Zahir Othman Ph.D.
Caroline Shaw
Ionis Thompson
Andrew Mead

Principal Originating Contributors

Contributors were attached to the organisations listed at the time of writing.

Professor Sir Norman Anderson, Institute of Advanced Legal Studies, University of London
H. St John Armitage, OBE
Dr Randall Baker, University of East Anglia
Jeremy Barnett and John Ewart, British Council, Riyadh
Dr Richard A. Chapman, University of Durham
Hajj D. Cowan, School of Oriental and African Studies, University of London
Peter Duncan, Stanford Research Institute, Riyadh
Dr Abdullah S. El-Banyan, Ministry of Labour and Social Affairs, Riyadh
Professor William Fisher, University of Durham
Dr Hassan H. Hajrah, King Abdul Aziz University, Jeddah
G.R. Hawting, School of Oriental and African Studies, University of London
Professor T.M. Johnstone, School of Oriental and African Studies, University of London
Dr Fadil K. Kabbani, Deputy Minister for Mineral Resources, Saudi Arabia
Dr Geoffrey King, School of Oriental and African Studies, University of London
James P. Mandaville, Saudi Arabian American Oil Company, Dhahran
Elizabeth Monroe, CMG, St Anthony's College, University of Oxford
Dr Theodore Prochazka, University of Riyadh
Dr Fazlur Rahman, University of Chicago
Dr George Rentz, Hoover Institution, Stanford, California
Cecile Rouchdy, Dar el-Hanan School, Jeddah
Dr Mahmoud Esma'il Sieny, The Arabic Language Institute, University of Riyadh
Dr Ibrahim Zaid, General Organization for Social Insurance, Saudi Arabia

Photographic Credits

Every effort has been made to contact the owners of copyright material. All images copyright Stacey International unless otherwise stated below. The following photographers and institutions are gratefully acknowledged for their contributions:

Turath: 2-3, 10-11, 22t, 23tb, 62, 65, 66, 68, 69, 70, 71, 72, 73, 74, 75, 76r, 102&103br, bl cr, 104, 106t&b, 107t&b, 110-1, 112, 113, 117, 124, 127l, 134b, 144-5, 148, 158-9, 168, 169, 170l&r, 171, 177t&b, 181, 205, 206-7, 220, 222, 223, 227t&bl, 228, 229(3), 230, 231t&b, 235b; Ministry of Information: 6,7, 76l, 77, 161, 163, 172-3; Gloria Kifayeh: 12, 150-1; Gunnar Bemert: 16t&b, 17, 53t, 128, 129, 141, 142, 147, 156-7b, 178b, 185tr&l, br, 186, 194, 195t, 202t, 203t&b, 215, 216-7, 221, 224r; Saudi Aramco World/PADIA:18, 59lr, 94, 96b, 99t&b, 103t, c, l, 109, 116, 127r, 156t, 123t&b, 138, 140t&b, 155r, 188t&b, 189t&b, 190b, 193t, 197, 198, 199t&b, 202b, 204t, 212(3), 213, 224l, 234; Alan Keohane: 19; John Pint: 20; Lars Bjurstrom: 21tmbr, 27, 28, 29t&b, 30, 31 (1-4), 32 (1-4), 33, 36(3), 90, 105, 118; Eric Moore 22 r(3) bl(2); H Jungius 24t, H & J Ericsson 26(2&3); John Stewart-Smith 26(4); Royal Geographical Society: 34, 50, 60, 61, 64t; Ionis

Thompson: 37, 66, 108, 235t; Department of Antiquities, Saudi Arabia: 39; Peter Harrigan: 40-41, 42, 43, 78-9, 180t; Middle East Archives: 49lr; John Herbert 53mb, 178t, 185bl, 214; John Topham: 81(6), 85, 86, 87br&l, 88, 89; Eric Bjurstrom: 83lr, 86, 87, 233; Peter Sanders: 92, 114-115, 119, 120-1, 122, 123, 146, 155bl, br, 157t, 164t&b, 166, 167, 225r; Donna Pepperdine: 126; Mohammd Shabeeb: 134t; Ali Mubarak: 136; Shell: 174; SABIC: 179; SABL: 192t&b, 193b; BAe: 210br&bl, 211; Getty Images: 226, 227br, 237.

Maps by Jennifer Skelley Cartographic Services

Contents

Introduction

This comprehensive work records an astonishing period in history of one of the most significant countries in the world as it emerged into modern statehood. When the bounty of Saudi Arabia's natural resources became evident soon after the mid point of the last century, the ancient land of Arabia under its Saudi leadership had various options. It chose to seize its opportunities and embrace its responsibilities both for the longer-term future and for the present, and on behalf of the Arab and Islamic communities, for whom the country is guardian of their most holy places. All of this speaks well of the Saudi Arabian people and their leadership.

King Faisal (1964-1975) laid the foundation of the country's domestic and foreign policy. He was a wise man, and devoted to the brotherhood of Muslims. Such wisdom and devotion dictated the development of social policy and investment in infrastructure at home, and guided relations with Islamic countries and the industrialised world. His policies were pursued by King Khalid (1975-1982), under whom the nation experienced a period of unprecedented prosperity.

From 1982, King Fahd's policy in domestic and foreign affairs continued to be rooted in the country's commitment to Islam from which, as he declared, "emanate all our ideals". During King Fahd's reign alone, the Kingdom's indigenous population nearly doubled. Even so, successive Five Year Plans brought radical improvements in the people's standard of

*Custodian of the Two Holy Mosques
King Abdullah ibn Abdul Aziz*

living, their welfare, social security, education and personal expecations, and so continue. For the young, both male and female, opportunities have opened such as would have astonished their grandparents at the same age. As for industrial production and agriculture, self-sufficiency became the goal, to secure the future with the planned husbandry of today's finite resources. In great measure this has been achieved.

Saudi Arabia's founding father, the late King Abdul Aziz ibn Saud, who died in 1953, established the principles of the country's foreign policy, namely peace and Islamic solidarity. It is a policy that has withstood severe tests, not least when Saudi Arabia and the fellow members of the Gulf Cooperation Council, together with forces from around the world, acted decisively in coming to the aid of Kuwait in 1991. More than a decade later, the Kingdom's influence for international stability was to prove vital when the region was shaken by renewed conflict and foreign intervention.

On the death of King Fahd in July 2005, his heir and brother, Crown Prince Abdullah succeeded to the throne. The new king had already served as de facto ruler during much of the previous ten years, owing to King Fahd's ill health. The accession of King Abdullah, charismatic and committed to maintaining the momentum of his country's development, was widely welcomed both domestically and by the international community.

HRH Prince Sultan ibn Abdul Aziz
Crown Prince of The Kingdom of Saudi Arabia

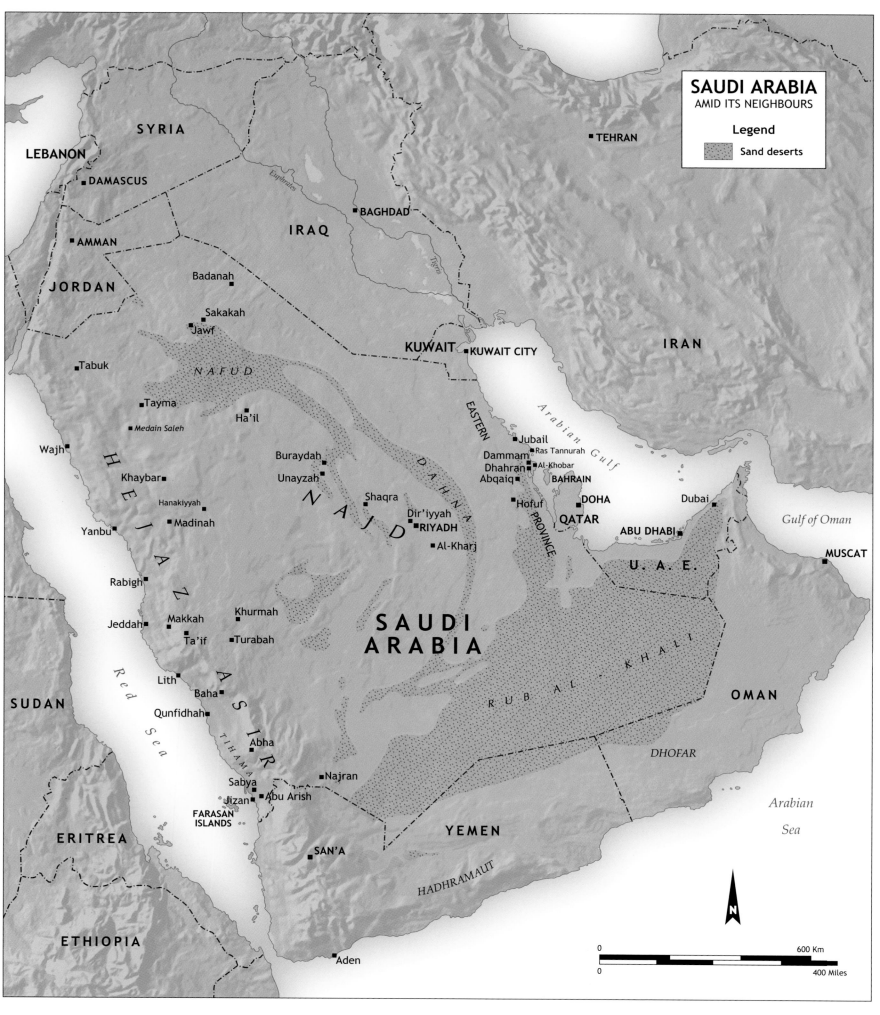

LEBANON

SYRIA

DAMASCUS

TEHRAN

AMMAN

JORDAN

BAGHDAD

IRAQ

Euphrates

Badanah

Sakakah

Jawf

Tabuk

N A F U D

KUWAIT

KUWAIT CITY

IRAN

Tayma

Ha'il

Medain Saleh

Wajh

H E J A Z

Khaybar

Buraydah

Unayzah

N A J D

Shaqra

D A H N A

Arabian Gulf

Jubail

Dammam   Ras Tannurah

Dhahran   Al-Khobar

Abqaiq

BAHRAIN

Hanakiyyah

Madinah

Dir'iyyah

RIYADH

Hofuf

DOHA

Dubai

Yanbu

Al-Kharj

PROVINCE

QATAR

ABU DHABI

Gulf of Oman

Rabigh

EASTERN

U. A. E.

MUSCAT

Makkah

Khurmah

Jeddah

Ta'if   Turabah

SAUDI
ARABIA

A S I R

Lith

R U B   A L   K H A L I

OMAN

Baha

T I H A M A

Qunfidhah

Abha

DHOFAR

Najran

Arabian

Sabya

Jizan   Abu Arish

FARASAN
ISLANDS

YEMEN

Sea

ERITREA

SAN'A

HADHRAMAUT

N

SUDAN

Red Sea

ETHIOPIA

Aden

| 0 | | | 600 Km |
| 0 | | | 400 Miles |

Maps

Historic Cartography

1

Geography and Geology

Expanses of loess and sand deserts dominate the landscape of much of the Arabian peninsula. Yet Saudi Arabian terrain varies dramatically, with dependably watered and fertile mountain slopes and valleys in the south-west. Oasis towns have immemorially drawn water from natural aquifers, most notably in the east and north. Spring rains can bring much of the arid plains spectacularly alive with plants and insect life.

The granite heights have withstood aeons of erosion to provide the desert landscape west of the capital city of Riyadh with the dramatic skyline of the Tuwayq escarpment.

The Arabian peninsula, of which the Saudi Arabian Kingdom forms by far the largest part, covers well over three million square kilometres (Saudi Arabia itself comprises 2,300,000 square kilometres – nearly 900,000 square miles). The whole peninsula is a fragment detached from the continent of Africa. Starting some 50 million years ago, thermal currents deep in the earth's mantle under Africa caused great rifts to form in the crust. These rifts have gradually widened in the ages since, and now comprise the Red Sea and the Gulf of Aden. More recently tectonic forces have caused the Arabian plate to tilt, with the western side upraised and the eastern side lowered. Shallow ancient seas covered the east, laying down layers of younger sedimentary rocks, and leading to the formation of oil deposits. In the west, volcanic disturbances led to much upwelling of magma which has, over the last ten million years, produced the extensive lava fields (*harrah*) that occur all along the west side of the country, mostly in the Makkah-Jeddah-Madinah area. With ancient igneous and metamorphic rocks in the west (the Arabian Shield, as it is known to geologists), capped here and there with more recent lava, and progressively younger rocks towards the east, Saudi Arabia exhibits in its geography, broadly speaking, a north-south running 'grain'. In the extreme west, along the Red Sea, there is a coastal plain (Tihama), flat and usually very narrow, except in the Jeddah area where it offers a small but useful lowland gap giving access to Makkah and the interior. Running north-south immediately to the east of Makkah is a formidable high plateau with a steep escarpment overlooking the Tihama below. Here occur the highest peaks in Saudi Arabia; particularly between Ta'if and Abha, where heights of 2,500 metres are reached. East again of this highland zone is an extensive region of irregular plateaux and upland basins, where collections of sub-surface water allows human settlement on a larger scale, as at

Left:

The Rub al-Khali, or Empty Quarter, is the largest sand mass on the Arabian peninsula, a huge swathe of shifting dunes.

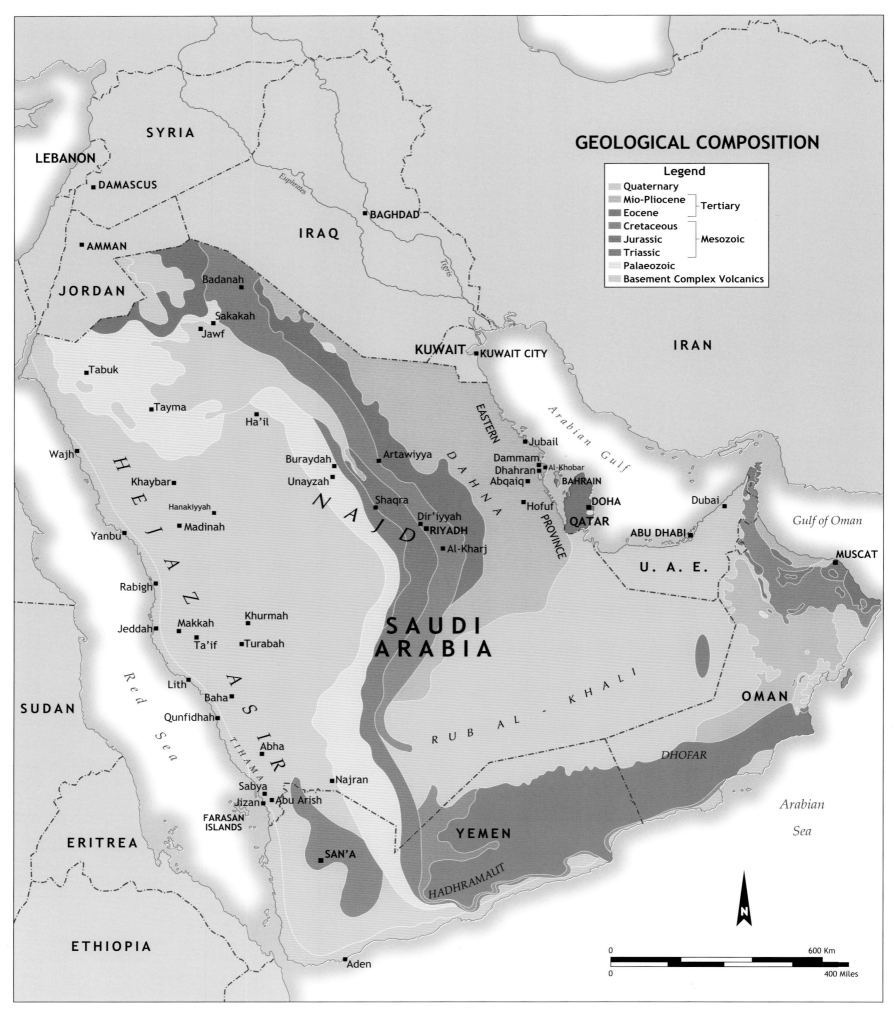

GEOLOGICAL COMPOSITION

Legend

Quaternary
Mio-Pliocene ⎤
Eocene ⎦ Tertiary
Cretaceous ⎤
Jurassic ⎥ Mesozoic
Triassic ⎦
Palaeozoic
Basement Complex Volcanics

LEBANON

SYRIA

DAMASCUS

AMMAN

JORDAN

IRAQ

BAGHDAD

Euphrates

Tigris

KUWAIT

KUWAIT CITY

IRAN

Badanah

Sakakah

Jawf

Tabuk

Tayma

Ha'il

Wajh

Khaybar

Hanakiyyah

Madinah

Yanbu

Buraydah

Unayzah

Artawiyya

Shaqra

Dir'iyyah

RIYADH

Al-Kharj

EASTERN
PROVINCE

DAHNA

Jubail

Dammam

Dhahran

Al-Khobar

Abqaiq

Hofuf

BAHRAIN

DOHA

QATAR

Dubai

ABU DHABI

U. A. E.

Arabian Gulf

Gulf of Oman

MUSCAT

HEJAZ

NAJD

Rabigh

Jeddah

Makkah

Ta'if

Khurmah

Turabah

SAUDI
ARABIA

Lith

Baha

Qunfidhah

ASIR

TIHAMA

Abha

Sabya

Jizan

Abu Arish

FARASAN
ISLANDS

Najran

RUB AL - KHALI

DHOFAR

OMAN

Arabian

Sea

SUDAN

Red
Sea

ERITREA

YEMEN

HADHRAMAUT

SAN'A

ETHIOPIA

Aden

N

0   600 Km

0   400 Miles

Above:

Between the immense sands of the Empty Quarter to the south and the sands of the Great Nafud to the north lie the sands of the Dahna, a great arc of dunes running over 1,000 km to join the two sand seas (see also map **opposite**). *The Dahna is characterised by the distinctive red hue of the sand, generally lying in rolling dunes.*

Madinah. Further east, altitude gradually declines, where occurs a whole succession of younger, sedimentary rocks, sandstones, limestones and marls. The harder series stand out as scarps or isolated ridges, with lower, flatter valleys formed in the less resistant strata between. The most imposing of these scarps is the Jabal Tuwayq, a limestone ridge that attains almost a thousand metres and extends in a sinuous curve northwest and southwest of Riyadh. Gradually, altitude diminishes eastwards, until one of the last of these scarps occurs near Hofuf, after which the surface drops to form the low-lying coastal plain of Hasa. Although some lowland areas or basins consist of bare rock pavement, most tend to be covered in loose rock deposits eroded by wind, by shattering due to temperature contrasts and, in the recent geological past, by water action. Near hill or plateau bases are stony areas of larger rock fragments; further away are outwash gravels, while in areas of low relief sand predominates, with silts in valley bottoms. Sand covers large areas. In the north, the Great Nafud is an expanse of sand dunes

(*uruq*), often reddish in colour, interspersed with areas of bare rock pavement. A narrower zone of sand, the Dahna, links the Great Nafud to an even larger expanse of sand, indeed the largest sand desert in the world, the Rub al-Khali or Empty Quarter, which occupies much of the south of Saudi Arabia. In the extreme west the Rub al-Khali is a 'sand sea' surrounded by gravel plains: in the east, there are massive dunes with salt flats (*sabkhah*). The whole area was for long an extreme hindrance to human movement, but oil prospecting and the discovery of artesian water have reduced the difficulty.

Of all the sizeable countries on earth, Saudi Arabia is probably the driest. It derives its weather mainly from the north and west: climatically it is linked to the eastern Mediterranean and adjacent lands, in that it has a long, hot and almost totally dry summer, with a short cool winter season during which a little rain occurs. This is because air masses reaching Arabia have been largely exhausted of their moisture. Although Arabia is surrounded on three sides by sea, aridity is the dominant

Left, below and opposite:

*The terracing system of agriculture is the only practical way to exploit the fertile soil on the steep slopes of the mountainous Asir region. Labour intensive, and requiring constant maintenance, it depends upon making maximum use of the seasonal rainwaters which are channelled from terrace to terrace, to run off into the valley (**below**). With cheap imported food and easier means of making a living, there has been some concern that this ancient method of farming might be neglected. A terraced farm will soon collapse and lead to erosion of the soil if not assiduously maintained. With care and skill, however, these mountain slopes can sustain the needs of local communities indefinitely (as **opposite**).*

feature. With the sole exception of Asir in the extreme southwest, any influences from the southern tropical zones are excluded by the highland rim that runs from Oman through the Hadhramaut to Yemen. Because of the dryness of the air reaching Saudi Arabia and the consequent lack of cloud, insulation is considerable, producing very high summer temperatures – up to 45° or 50°C – and sometimes even more in the southern deserts. But the cloudlessness also allows heat to escape from the surface at night, especially in winter, so temperatures drop quite markedly between day and night, and between summer and winter. The night coolness, with a 10° to 22°C drop at both seasons, is a boon in summer but leads to sporadic frost in the interior of the centre and north during winter; temperatures as low as -7°C have been recorded at Riyadh. Rainfall is irregular and unreliable, occurring mostly during the months from October to April. Except along the southern Red Sea coast, and inland over the mountains of Asir, summers are practically rainless, and in the interior several years may

Water

Until the 1980s, Saudi Arabia had lakes at Layla Aflaj and deep waterholes at al-Kharj and elsewhere, fed by huge underground aquifers, formed in prehistoric times and non-renewable. Al-Kharj, pictured here in the days before the water was completely depleted, was a valuable source of drinking water in an otherwise barren terrain. In recent years, these aquifers have been drawn upon heavily, both for agricultural and domestic purposes, and no fresh water remains in the lakes or pits.

The government is aware of the problem and has developed a water strategy that focuses on supplying the ever-increasing requirement from renewable sources. The re-use of wastewater for agricultural purposes will prevent some of the drain on the valuable groundwater reserves, and fresh water will increasingly be supplied from desalination plants, of which there are currently 27 in the Kingdom, with three more planned. Leakage, a universal problem receiving increasing attention in water management, is also being addressed and can have a dramatic impact in reducing the need to draw on precious reserves. The government is working to spread public awareness of the importance of conserving water and rationing its consumption. While Arabia's desert dwellers of fifty years ago would have treasured water probably more than any other people on the face of the earth, the new generation has come to take the supply of fresh water for granted, a trend that needs to be reversed if the underground aquifers are not to be completely exhausted.

Right:
The water at al-Kharj wells up from subterranean aquifers, previously a valuable source of good drinking water in an otherwise barren terrain.

---

elapse without rain. The extreme south of Saudi Arabia, the virtually uninhabited Rub al-Khali, is almost entirely without rain – one of the driest areas on earth; but over the rest of the country (Asir excepted) annual rainfall amounts to about 100 mm, though 150 mm have been known to fall locally within twenty-four hours. Because of temperature contrasts winds can be strong, even violent, raising dust storms from time to time. On the coasts humidity is high, due to moist sea breezes. This effect is, however, local, and most of the interior is extremely dry. The mean figures given on page 16 illustrate the principal features of the Saudi Arabian climate, as well as the contrasts between coast and interior. The hills of Asir, however, receive the marked summer rainfall which benefits the Yemen plateau. Until recently the difficulty of the terrain, its aridity and the consequent scarcity of good soil sharply controlled the ways of life within Saudi Arabia.

Before the discovery of oil, about a quarter of the population was wholly nomadic, following a regular pattern of rough grazing of sheep, goats and camels, which involved considerable annual movement and making use of the wells which then tapped the underground aquifers. In recent years this source has dramatically declined (*see box*) and true nomadism has much reduced: in central Arabia it is still common to see communities with black goat-hair tents, but these tend increasingly to be settled and supplied by water tanker, and their tents are gradually being replaced by concrete houses.

Opposite:
The nomadic peoples of Arabia had a store of inherited knowledge that guided them to vital sources of water. Far fewer of these peoples exist today, having settled in the towns or villages where piped water obviates the need to quest the desert sands. There are, however, still some who depend for sustenance on their roving herds of goats, and also camels.

Left:
The cave being surveyed here is some 50 million years old, formed in an age when the Arabian peninsula was much wetter and probably had permanent drainage.

Opposite:
As the water table dropped, these caves emptied. Continued dripping of rainwater and remaining aquifers still brought minute mineral deposits, giving rise to stalactites and stalagmites as well as beautiful crystal formations.

Caves

Beneath the harsh deserts of Saudi Arabia lie dark chambers and complex mazes filled with crystalline structures *(left, and below left)*, stalactites and stalagmites *(below)*. The limestone floor of the Summan plateau, a karst area to the east of the Dahna sands, is riddled with such caves, known locally as *dahls*. Some have tiny entrances which open into wider caves, others lead into a maze of passages which can be several kilometres long.

Essential to the formation of these underground cavities is the action of water percolating through soluble rock. The process is slow. Rainwater absorbs fractional amounts of carbon dioxide from the air as it falls, making a weak carbonic acid solution that eats into the limestone and eventually forms hollows and channels.

Local Bedouin have always known of these caves and some have obviously been used as water supplies. First systematically studied in the 1980s, they are currently being explored, surveyed and reported by the Saudi Geological Survey.

Flora and Fauna

Maps and geography books make Arabia a part of Asia, but plant and animal life clearly bear out the theory that it is really an extension of Africa. The desert steppes which now link the peninsula with Asia are the bottom of an ancient sea which once divided the continents. The animals and plants of northern and north-eastern Saudi Arabia are generally closely related to or identical with Saharan species. To the south and the west, wildlife assumes its older, tropical African character.

Plant Life

Except in parts of the Asir highlands, where juniper, wild olive, and some other larger trees grow together over large areas, there are no forests in Saudi Arabia. In some parts, scattered small acacia trees are common. Further east and north the vegetation is typical of arid steppes – hundreds of square kilometres of small, drought-adapted shrubs, a metre or less high. Often one species, such as the *rimth* saltbush or the yellow-flowered *arfaj* shrublet, dominates the landscape. The ground between these shrublets is green for only two to three months of the year, when winter rains bring forth a host of herbs. Among these annuals, known collectively as *usht* by the Bedouin, are the desert *Anthemis* or camomile, many species of the mustard family, and a striking iris. Only the salt-impregnated bottoms of *sabkhahs*, small areas of rock-floored desert, and a few fields of actively moving dunes do not support any plants. Even most parts of the Rub al-Khali have scattered shrublets of the prickly *hadh* saltbush, a tribulus, or the scarlet-fruited *abal*.

Clockwise from above right:
*The flowering hibiscus, the marigold (*calendula officinalis*), pomegranate, frangipani, bougainvillaea, and the lilly-like* Datura stramonium.

Opposite:
Ghaf *tree. Of the acacia family, its elongated pods supply fodder for animals.*

Left:

Mainly nocturnal, the desert hare is one of the most versatile mammals on the peninsula. Though hunted by man, wild cats, wolves and foxes, it survives in considerable numbers.

Below:

The Arabian oryx, inspiration for the mythical unicorn, became extinct in the wild in 1972 due to over-hunting. Re-introduced from animals in reservations abroad, a thriving herd is today protected by a large Saudi wildlife park.

Mammals

The landscape of the Arabian peninsula, with its harsh extremes of heat and cold and its apparent absence of dependable food sources, might suggest no very significant mammal habitation. The opposite is true. Arabia historically has sustained a wide variety of mammal species, several unique to the peninsula, having adapted by evolution to the demands of the climate. Some such species survive by the merest thread today.

A dramatic story of the recent rescue of an important species of large mammal is that of the Arabian oryx. This 100-kilogram antelope – by far the largest wild mammal in Saudi Arabia – with its long, straight horns, was known in this area in Biblical times, but became extinct in the wild by the early 1960s. A successful breeding and reintroduction programme was undertaken by the National Wildlife Research Centre near Ta'if, and has re-established native herds. Starting with a founder population of just 54 in 1995, there are now about 200 Arabian oryx living and breeding in the Empty Quarter. Despite sporadic hunting, and other initial problems, this number has been maintained for several years and it is now possible for the traveller crossing the sands of southern Saudi Arabia suddenly to glimpse one of these magnificent beasts outlined against the sky on a distant ridge or dune.

The graceful *reem* or sand gazelle and the rarer *idmi*, or mountain gazelle, and the *afri*, or Saudi gazelle, used to be seen throughout Arabia but became extinct in the wild by about 1990. The breeding programme at KKWRC, (the King Khalid Wildlife Research Centre) at Thumamah, near Riyadh, however, has successfully bred and reintroduced numbers of both species of gazelle into the Empty Quarter. The *reem*, which thrive on sand and live in large herds, are now thought to number about one thousand. The *idmi*, which live in smaller family groups and prefer rocky terrain, are fewer in number and are now living all along the Tuwaiq escarpment south of Qaryat al-Fao, covering an area of about 1,000 square kilometres.

The Saudi gazelle and the Mountain gazelle

survive in small pockets, and in the Farasan Islands. The ibex, a large wild goat often depicted in rock art, never entirely disappeared from the wild. It is now protected from hunting in a Protected Area, Wadi Howtah beni Tammim, some 200 kilometres south of Riyadh, where its numbers remain steady. The Arabian cheetah, smaller than its African cousin, and with a whiter pelt, is probably now extinct. It is possible that the caracal lynx still exists in the north.

The Arabian leopard population, surviving mainly in the highlands of Asir, has declined drastically in recent years and may now be as low as 100 in the entire Arabian peninsula. Whatever population that still exists lives a shy and retiring existence in the remoter reaches of the Asir mountains, away from man, its only predator. The Arabian sand cat, smaller than the domestic cat but similar to it in appearance, can occasionally be glimpsed in barren sand country. The Arabian wolf, *canis lupus arabicus*, jackals, foxes, and the striped hyena are found in Arabia, as are the hedgehog, the porcupine and the *ratel*, or honey badger.

Above:

The reem, *the largest of the Arabian gazelles, does not leap or bound, but runs with neck stretched out at an astonishing pace. Although diminished in numbers in recent years, it is still to be seen in herds of up to a hundred.*

Left from top:

The familiar hoopoe is revered in Islam for its beauty and the symbolism of the bismillah *implied by its elegant beak.*

The gregarious Arabian golden sparrow is mostly restricted to the southwest, but it can be found there in large flocks.

The Chestnut-bell Sandgrouse is nicknamed the 'butcher bird' because of its habit of impaling its prey on long thorns before tearing it apart.

The handsome little green bee-eater is one of the more colourful and widespread of Arabian residents. It is most commonly seen on the acacia bush from which it darts to catch flying insects.

Opposite:

The white heron lives and flourishes off the western coast of Saudi Arabia feeding on the fish of the Red Sea.

Birds

Several million birds, including flamingoes, storks, swallows, wagtails and warblers, pass through Arabia on their spring and autumn migrations, some staying over winter. Among the true desert residents are six species of sand grouse and several larks, including the sweet-voiced hoopoe lark, known to the desert Arab as *Umm Salim* (Salim's Mother). Game birds in Saudi Arabia include the houbara bustard (a large bird very popular with hunters using falcons) the curlew and the courser. The houbara is being bred in captivity for later release into the wild at the National Wildlife Research Centre south of Taif. It has been progressively released within the Protected Areas since 1991 and its numbers have now greatly increased. The Arabian ostrich has disappeared but a similar species, the red-necked ostrich, is also being bred at the NWRC and released into the wild. The Arabian helmeted guineafowl now occurs naturally only in the area around Jizan but a captive population has been established at the NWRC in order to maintain the genetic purity of this Arabian bird.

Among the birds of prey are harriers, buzzards, imperial and steppe eagles and falcons which are often trained to catch hares and houbara. Flocks of brilliantly-coloured bee-eaters and parakeets, escaped from private collections, can be seen over gardens and agricultural areas, where they are probably now resident. Water birds, such as ibises, herons, egrets, gulls and pelicans inhabit the rich tropical coastal areas.

The bird population, both resident and visiting, changes continuously. New wetland habitats, such as the 50 kilometres of treated waste-water called the Riyadh River, have become rich environments sustaining vegetation, fish and now migratory birds. These have been encouraged to stop briefly, to over-winter, and in some cases to breed. The species spotted there include pelicans, kingfishers, greylag geese and large numbers of herons and black-winged stilts.

Above:

The smooth-scaled sand boa is particularly well adapted to its environment, eyes and nostrils placed well up on the head so that it can bury itself in the sand and await its prey.

Right:

A gecko is frozen into immobility against the light shining through a stalagmite.

Opposite:

Agamids abound in the Arabian desert. As reptiles, their body temperature is maintained by exposure to the sun where necessary, rather than depending on burning the food resource as mammals do. This makes them often more efficient in the desert where there is plenty of sun but a shortage of food, especially as most need very little water to survive.

Reptiles

The water-conserving body structure of reptiles makes them well adapted for life in arid lands, but many cannot endure extremes of heat and are obliged to lead nocturnal or subterranean lives. Thus, although some 14 species of snake have been reported in Saudi Arabia, few are seen. One of the venomous snakes of Arabia, the sand viper or horned viper, is found lurking beneath the sand in most parts of the peninsula. Two carpet vipers are found; the common carpet viper in the southern steppes and Burton's carpet viper (so named for its carpet-like markings) in moist wadis. More dangerous are the rare black cobra of the northeast, the Arabian cobra of the southwest and the puff adder. Harmless snakes are common, among them the long elegant racer, the glossy-bellied racer and the cliff racer. Jayakar's sand boa has no venom but suffocates its prey. One of the most venomous of all, the sea snake, is found in the waters of the Gulf: fortunately it is quite pacific. There are no poisonous lizards in Arabia, although two species are imposingly large – the 60-centimetre long, plant-eating *dhub*, (hunted for food and now endangered) and the longer monitor lizard which can measure as much as 150 centimetres in length. There are two species of agamid in Arabia, over 30 species of gecko and several types of skink and lacertid lizards.

Marine Life

The coral reefs of the Arabian peninsula are among the most beautiful in the world. Their abundant marine life is breathtaking in its designs and vibrant colours. Indeed, this underwater paradise is so undisturbed – except of course near ports – that underwater visitors to the reef can think of themselves as pioneers, for few areas have been well explored. The most rewarding time of day to see this world is in early morning or late afternoon, when many creatures emerge from their hiding places to nibble at plant life and hunt prey.

The Red Sea is comparatively unpolluted, hence the richness of its marine life. Though classified as part of the Indo-Pacific region, it is somewhat isolated from that larger area of water. Various unique species have evolved there, though their close relations can often be found along the Indian Ocean coasts of Yemen, Socotra and Oman, and, with less certainty, in the Gulf. Coral provides the vital protective environment.

Usually separated from the shore by a shallow sandy channel, the edge of the reef flat drops away suddenly. Here, on its almost sheer face, are to be found many of the constantly growing organisms: the fire coral with its painful sting, the massive brain coral, and the delicate web-like red gorgonian coral, amongst others. The extraordinary structures of these corals provide homes and hiding places for the various inhabitants of the reef, which include sea urchins, anemones, starfish, slugs, squid, crustaceans, and molluscs, as well as a wealth of tropical fish. Creating an impression of constantly changing colour and movement, they jointly make up the carefully balanced ecosystem of the reef.

Spectacular inhabitants of the reef are the brilliantly coloured fish: the butterfly fish, coralfish, clownfish, parrotfish and angelfish. Their often bizarre shapes are perfectly adapted to their lifestyles and habitats. But their glowing colours and designs – reds, pinks, oranges, yellows, blues and greens in spotted, dotted, checked, stripped or splashed patterns – create a complex marine riddle. Nowadays most marine zoologists believe that these lavish markings constitute, primarily, a form of sign language to indicate territorial rights and warn other individuals of the same species against entering their territory. The markings also facilitate the finding of a mate in a densely populated habitat.

Although there are many friendly and harmless fish to be seen, the reef's inhabitants include some extremely dangerous creatures. Of these, some of the most poisonous make full use of their camouflage abilities. Both the scorpionfish and stonefish lurk in wait for victims, disguised as rough pieces of algae-covered rock. If the stonefish is stepped on, and one of its thirteen dorsal spines punctures a blood vessel, death can occur in an hour.

All the marine creatures of the reef play a part in the underwater balance of life. The interdependent relationships of the different species are complex and fascinating. Underpinning it all, however, is the reef itself, a living organic structure built up over long periods and stretching up the Red Sea, providing a habitat and security for the marine life around it. Marine biologists are, however, insistant that the reef is under threat, and are increasingly alarmed by the fact. All coral reefs flourish only within a narrow band of temperatures. Global warming, with consequently higher water temperatures, has already placed in hazard much of the world's reef habitat. If this is set to continue, the nature of the sea life off the western coast of Saudi Arabia will change beyond recognition within a few decades.

The reefs of the Red Sea coast bear witness to an astonishing array of the inventiveness of the sea's inhabitants.

Right, from top:

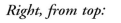

Royal angelfish, anemone, hawkfish, soldierfish.

Opposite:

Jewel fish are a common sight for scuba divers of the west coast.

Left:
*Spiders (as the black widow spider, **far left**) and beetles (as the domino beetle, **left**) are particularly abundant in the desert because of their ability to withstand the extreme heat and drought.*

*Scorpions (**left**) inhabit the Arabian deserts in large numbers, shading from the sun beneath rocks. Their sting, although extremely painful, is rarely fatal.*

*The praying mantis, camouflaged in the green vegetation awaits its unsuspecting prey (**far left**).*

Insects and Arachnids

An insect evocative of Arabia through ancient legend is the desert locust. It is found across that great swathe of arid territory that stretches from the western Sahara to southwest Pakistan. When not swarming, it occurs in the drier central part of the desert, where it survives by migrating. During plagues it invades larger surrounding fertile areas, reaching East Africa, the Fertile Crescent, and even southern Europe. 'Invades' is the word, for until recently a plague of locusts could devastate entire regions, all green growth at the mercy of the locusts' appetite. Yet the locust is no different in this respect from any migratory animal – it must migrate to where the rain has fallen and fresh vegetation is growing, or it dies. The desert locust still has the potential to swarm and ravage crops but its movements are now monitored and controlled. The last upsurge in locust numbers in the region was in 1996, but this was soon brought under control. Mosquitoes, another source of woe for man owing to the malaria they carry, have been wiped out by Government campaigns in most urban districts.

Among the more common insects to be seen in the desert are the shiny black dung or scarab beetle which lays its eggs on balls of animal dung; and the carabid ground beetle, commonly known as the domino beetle from its colouring. There are several species of scorpion, all very poisonous, and the large, non-venomous camel spider, which hunts at night. No fewer than 147 varieties of butterflies and numerous moths can be seen in Arabia. Noteworthy are the beautiful painted lady, the African lime swallowtail and the oleander hawk-moth.

Conservation

Islamic teachings enjoin the need to set aside areas by settlements and keep them free from grazing or depredation in order to preserve certain animals or food sources for man's use. These areas, which have been managed since

Opposite:
In rainy years, huge numbers of the painted lady breed in the Arabian desert zone. It is by far the most widely distributed of the world's butterflies. As a versatile migrant it may suddenly occur in numbers in habitats where it cannot survive on a permanent basis.

early Islamic times, are known as *himas* (a word which often occurs in place-names). They have set aside areas for example, for honey production and crops for times of drought, and in some areas animals have also been protected from hunting. From these early roots have arisen the new national parks, known as Protected Areas. There are currently 15 of these throughout the Kingdom. They include the Harrat al-Harrah in the northwest of Saudi Arabia (established in 1987), where the houbara bustards were released, the Farasan Islands (1989), Mahazat as-Sayd,

(1988) and Uruq Bani Ma'arid (1994), both on the edge of the Empty Quarter, where the Arabian oryx were released. Within these areas hunting and grazing are forbidden. A further 41 terrestrial and 47 marine sites have been identified as worthy of protection but the establishment of these as Protected Areas will proceed slowly.

There are two research stations within the Kingdom for breeding endangered species and reintroducing them into the wild. The King Khalid Wildlife Research Centre (KKWRC) near Riyadh was founded in 1987 to develop

the private animal collection of the late King Khalid. Since then the collection has been hugely expanded. Most non-Arabian animals have been removed and research is concentrated on the native species of Arabian oryx, and the gazelles *idmi* and *reem*. Research into their diseases is part of the work of the Centre. The captive herd of Arabian oryx is now kept at the National Wildlife Research Centre (NWRC) near Ta'if. The National Ibex Reserve is situated in Wadi Howtah Beni Tammim and within it *idmi* are also released and monitored.

2

Pre-History and History

Arabia has a rich pre-Islamic past whose cultures and civilisations are only today being uncovered by archaeologists. Here it was that Islam was revealed to the Prophet Muhammad, whereafter the country became the focus and centre of the swiftly spreading new religion.

As for the Saudi Arabia we know today, its formation began only at the start of the twentieth century, through the vision and daring of the young Ibn Saud – later King Abdul Aziz. He restored the fortunes of the House of Saud which, since the mid-eighteenth century, had ruled much of central Arabia.

The camel-borne warriors of the youthful Abdul Aziz Ibn Saud struck fear (with Allah's holy allegiance embroidered on their flag) into those who would perpetuate colonial presence in east and central Arabia, up to the defeat of the Ottomans in the First World War. Captain William Shakespear captured the scene with his box camera in 1913.

Rock Art

The petroglyphs of Arabia lay uncharted until recently, but the country is now acknowledged as one of the richest regions in the world for rock art, with South Africa, Australia, India and Kazakhstan.

The hunting scenes depicted on the rocks at Jubbah, in the Nafud desert, some as much as 9,000 years old, show a way of life very different from the Bedouin traditions that evolved in the later hotter climatic period. Ostriches roamed a fertile terrain, and camels consistently appear, possible evidence that there once existed wild herds, as today there are still Bactrian camels in Central Asia.

The age of these petroglyphs is seldom easy to determine. The oldest have been long exposed to the process of patination, leaving the images with a deeper shade and closer to the colour of the rockface. As a general rule, the more clearly discernable the image, the more recent the engraving. The art is always concise, and often formalized. Some capture the creatures' grace and motion with seeming ease. The later images appear to lose this skill and are generally more coarsely executed.

The images on the rock faces in Jubbah, and elsewhere across the Kingdom, are now being catalogued and researched by Saudi Arabia's Department of Antiquities, which is committed to fostering a deeper understanding of the country's ancient history.

Palaeolithic

Man appeared in Arabia very early owing to the proximity of its western coast to the cradle of mankind, the Rift Valley of Africa. Tools dating from about one million years ago have been found near Shuwayhitiyah in the Northern Region and in the south near Najran, the work of *homo erectus*, ancestor of modern man. After about 500,000 years ago these simple shapes gave way to the more sophisticated handaxe of the Acheulian culture. Thousands of examples of these have been found in many parts of the Kingdom, fashioned from whatever hard stone was locally available, for example flint or quartzite in Najd, and basalt, quartzite and flint in the Empty Quarter, carried there by two of the great rivers of ancient Arabia, the Wadi Dawasir and the Wadi Sahba. Sometime after 100,000 years ago, when *homo erectus* had been over-taken by Neanderthal man, with his greater brain capacity, a new sort of stone tool technology appeared, the blade struck off a core and worked into points and scrapers (the Levallois technique). Neanderthal sites are thinly scattered around Arabia reflecting a small population in a time of increasing aridity. Then, about 35,000 years ago Neanderthal man mysteriously disappeared from the scene and a wet period encouraged his rival, *homo sapiens*, our direct ancestor, to populate Arabia in greater numbers. Fresh water lakes appeared at Yabrin, Layla, Al-Hasa and in the Empty Quarter, the Rub al-Khali. Big game, buffalo and antelope were hunted on prairies, hippos inhabited the lakes. About 17,000 BC these lakes dried up, the animals disappeared and the present day deserts of Arabia were formed. Man retreated to reappear in large numbers only with the next wet phase after about 9000 BC, when the lakes again filled with water and the grasslands reappeared.

Neolithic

This time man brought a new culture, the Neolithic, which reached Arabia earlier than Europe and was not exclusively associated with agriculture as in Europe. In Arabia, Neolithic man was both a pastoralist keeping herds of cows, sheep and goats and also a hunter-gatherer. He hunted gazelle and smaller animals and birds with his precision-chipped new tools, and abundant examples of arrowheads and spearheads lie scattered on the sand. Grindstones on Neolithic sites may indicate cultivation of cereals in some lakeshore settlements.

Rock art appears at this time, the earliest probably dating from about 7000 BC at Jubbah, north of Ha'il, and Hanakiyyah, near Madinah. Beautiful examples of this early art can be seen today. Saudi Arabia is exceptionally rich in rock art and it tells an interesting story: from it we learn a great deal about the people who inhabited the desert then, their dress, the animals they hunted and those they domesticated. Beautifully incised and naturalistic depictions of the animals hunted or herded are found particularly in the north around Jubbah and all down the west side of Arabia, around Bir Hima, Jebel Qara and Najran especially. At first cattle are most often shown, with long curving horns, and later ostrich, onagers, lions, camels, both hunted and domestic, Arabian ibex and oryx. The early rock art is the most naturalistic, particularly around Jubbah. Here and elsewhere religious ritual is visible in rock art in the form of priest-like figures carrying bowls, sometimes wearing tails and sacrificing cows. At Hanakiyyah on an unusual red rock near Madinah is an early depiction of a procession of animals. Elsewhere hunters can be seen carrying bows and arrows, spears and shields and wearing feather headdresses, skirts and jewellery. The women depicted on rocks, always with long hair, are sometimes associated with men in dances or rituals; sometimes they are alone and probably represent deities. The upraised hands indicate worship. Other evidence of Neolithic man seen all over the desert, especially on ridges and prominent on skylines, are cairns and tumuli: rough piles of stones or well-built circular structures, sometimes within a circular wall and often with "tails" or lines of stones interspersed with smaller cairns leading away from the main cairn along the contours of the slopes. These date from the

Above:

The standing stones of al-Rajajil *of the Jawf region are thought to represent the figures of men (from which the name Rajajil is derived) but these structures of the fourth century BC are still a source of mystery to archaeologists.*

Opposite:

This carved male figure is of white limestone of Sumerian origin (c.2700 BC). It stands about a metre tall, and was found on Tarut Island.

Below:

A Dilmun-type amphora from the third millennium BC, found on Tarut.

Bottom:

A large storage jar from Abqaiq, c.2500 BC.

Neolithic through to the Iron Age and are evidence of the increasing care associated with burial, and a growing religious consciousness and belief in an after-life.

Other stone structures have puzzled travellers and archaeologists. Long quadrangular "kites" are thought to have been for trapping animals. Stone circles are often associated with cairns and tumuli and their purpose probably varied: some perhaps were habitations, others funerary in purpose. At Rajajil near Sakakah is a fine set of 50 groups of standing stones. Each group consists of two to ten pillars, the highest of which is ten feet. A religious purpose is probable and a date of late fourth millennium BC. Meanwhile, in the land between the Tigris and Euphrates rivers, Mesopotamia, north of the Arabian Gulf, centres like Ubaid, Ur and Erech were developing and growing at a rapid pace, to emerge by about 3000 BC as the Middle East's first cities. Ever since the sixth millennium BC had come attractive pottery from Ubaid, exported down the Gulf in reed boats lined with bitumen to settlements along the coast from Kuwait to Oman. Ubaid pots have been found at many sites in Eastern Arabia, such as Dosariyah near Jubail.

All down the Gulf and Red Sea coasts gleaming white mounds indicate shell midden sites, the visible evidence of villages which existed along this coast from the sixth to the second millennia BC. The inhabitants lived on fish from the sea and shell-fish from lagoons lined with mangrove trees.

Bronze Age Towns & Trade
Third to first millennium BC

The Mesopotamian cities grew and their inhabitants, the Sumerians, learned how to manufacture bronze. However they lacked various basic materials needed, especially copper and wood, which had to be imported. From records left by the earliest form of writing, cuneiform, made by the impress of reed wedges on clay tablets, we learn of this trade: copper which was needed to make bronze was imported from the land they called Magan, the mountains of today's Oman, and wood and other commodities from Meluhha, the ancient

civilisation of the Indus Valley. A trading civilisation named Dilmun, mentioned in texts from as early as the late fourth millennium BC, grew up based on its entrepôt function for these goods. At first Dilmun was probably situated on the eastern Arabian mainland, in Hasa. Later, by the early third millennium BC, it was centred on the island of Bahrain. In the third and second millennia BC trade was flourishing up and down the Gulf and Dilmun grew rich. It made its own pottery and seals with lively scenes of everyday life and mythology, which were exported. The inhabitants of Dilmun buried their dead in stone tumuli which can be seen in huge numbers on Bahrain and also on the mainland of eastern Arabia as far inland as Yabrin. Thousands of tumuli once ringed the Dammam Dome. An important Dilmun centre was sited on the island of Tarut, off Qatif, where a mound now crowned by a Portuguese fort probably covers Arabia's first town. Here a fine Sumerian-type statue dating from the early third millennium has been found and some lovely steatite fragments, showing eagles and other creatures.

Arabia Before Islam
First millennium BC to sixth century AD

In the first millennium BC the western side of Arabia was gradually being drawn into the trade conducted by the burgeoning incense-based kingdoms of south Arabia, namely Saba, Ma'in, Qataban and Himyar. Frankincense and myrrh, produced in the monsoon-watered mountains of Dhofar, were much sought after by Egypt and later by Rome for personal fragrance and increasingly elaborate funerary rituals. The cities of the southern kingdoms conveyed this incense northwards along overland routes which forked at Najran, going either north through Asir or east via Qaryat al-Fao across the edge of the great Rub al-Khali desert, following wells and then the oases of Aflaj and Kharj either to ports on the east coast like the lost city of Gerrha or westward via the fertile area around modern Riyadh, then called Yamamah, north to Tayma. Many places in Arabia grew rich on this trade. Qaryat al-Fao, south of Sulayyil, was a flourishing town between the second century BC and the third

The Nabateans, the Arabic-speaking tribe who rose to prominence in the third century BC grew rich from the lucrative frankincense trade that ran from Dhofar to the Western Mediterranean and to Rome. Their territory straddled the trade's west Arabian route. Initially nomadic, they used the profit from this trade to settle and establish two major trading centres, Petra (in modern day Jordan) and Medain Saleh, (**above**), in today's Saudi Arabia.

*The trading centres of Petra and Medain Saleh were thriving towns. Of the peoples' dwellings, however, nothing remains. It is for their pastiche classical façades cut out of the living rock and excavated chambers that the cities are remembered. What is thought to be the grain store (**right**) is beside the funnelled "siq", similar to the entrance at Petra, and leading to the portentious façade and its chamber (**opposite**).*

AD when, as capital of the tribal confederation of Kindah, it traded goods from South Arabia north: some beautiful objects have been discovered there showing Egyptian, Hellenistic and Assyrian influence. Kindah represents the first recorded unification within Arabia of the tribes around the central authority of a common chief, a precedent for what the Prophet Mohammad later achieved in Hejaz. It became powerful enough even to mint its own coins. Kindah reached its apogee in the sixth century when it controlled large parts of Arabia, including Yamamah. In the Eastern Province, the city of Thaj has yielded quantities of figurines and some lovely gold and bronze objects from burials, showing a strong Roman influence. Gerrha, whose whereabouts is not exactly known but probably lay in Al-Hasa, was described by Pliny and Strabo as a large city with a wealth of gold and silver articles: according to them its houses were made of salt and its doors and ceilings were decorated with ivory, gold, silver and precious stones. The incense trade through Asir and Hejaz was in the late centuries BC

captured by an Arabic-speaking nomadic tribe, the Nabataeans. By extracting tolls for the goods passing through their area they became wealthy, settled and built their capital at Petra (now Wadi Musa in Jordan) and their second city, Medain Saleh, near al-Ula in Arabia. Both were huge bustling centres with caravans converging in their market places and rock-cut tombs in the rocks behind. These constitute the main part of what we see today. In Medain Saleh the tombs were cut into the sandstone jebels and their stepped pediments show Asiatic and Hellenistic influence.

The nearby oasis town of al-Ula had an earlier origin than Medain Saleh as the capital of the Dedanites and Lihyanites. It was also an important stop on the incense route and at one time the Sabaeans had their northern headquarters there. Minaean tombs, two surmounted by lions, appear as holes in the cliff-face behind the town. Large Lihyanite statues have been discovered here. Rock inscriptions of South Arabian traders are found all along the old incense routes, written in south and north Arabian scripts.

From the north of Arabia came groups of Arabs who harassed the caravans of the mighty Assyrian Empire in the seventh century BC. That they had limited success in this is indicated by a record of tribute exacted from Arab chiefs by Assyrian kings. Tayma, with its huge city walls dating to 1000 BC, was an important centre on the trade routes and in the sixth century BC achieved fame as the provincial capital of the last Neo-Babylonian king, Nabonidus. The famous Tayma stone stele, written in Aramaic and dating from the fifth century BC, was found in a well at Tayma.

Roman writers divided Arabia into Felix (modern south-western Saudi Arabia and Yemen), Petraea (the Nabataean kingdom) and Deserta (the rest). They made attempts to control the incense routes, most notably with Aelius Gallus' doomed expedition into Yemen in 24 BC but all failed until in the first century AD they discovered how to navigate the Red Sea, thus avoiding the dues exacted along the land route. Arabia Petraea became the Roman province of Arabia in AD 106. The Roman Governor of Arabia in the second century AD left a historic inscription in both Nabataean and Greek on the walls of a temple at Rawwafa, south-west of Tabouk. With the Romans' command of the Red Sea trade and the decreasing demand for incense following the advent of Christianity (when for a period the use of incense was prohibited), the direction of Roman trade swung from a south-north to a west-east axis. As a result, there was an economic slump in the south-west of Arabia from the third century AD and many tribes migrated north to the central region. *The Periplus of the Erythraean Sea*, a Greek geographer's account dated 50-60 AD, is the first record of organised trading with the east in vessels built and commanded by subjects of a western power and it marks the beginning of a new era.

By the eve of Islam most of the inhabitants of the Hejaz were largely settled in towns. For a time in the sixth century AD the Christian Abyssinians controlled Yemen and Najran (also Christian at that time) and their leader, Abraha, with his elephant, even threatened Makkah in 571, the year of the Prophet's birth. The local inhabitants' first sight of an elephant was

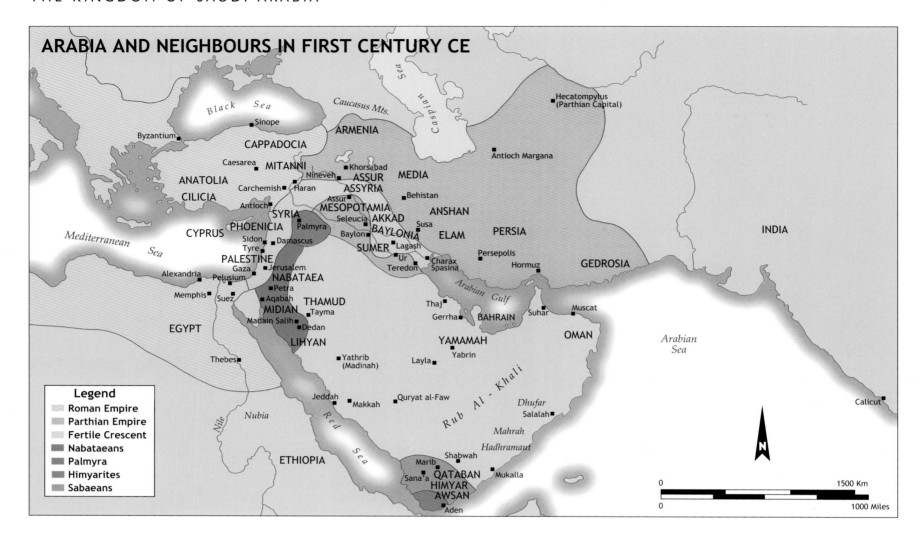

The map is titled "ARABIA AND NEIGHBOURS IN FIRST CENTURY CE" with the following labels:

Black Sea, Caucasus Mts., Caspian Sea, Sinope, Byzantium, CAPPADOCIA, ARMENIA, Hecatompylus (Parthian Capital), Caesarea, MITANNI, Khorsabad, MEDIA, Antioch Margana, ANATOLIA, Carchemish, Haran, Nineveh, ASSUR, ASSYRIA, Behistan, CILICIA, Antioch, Assur, MESOPOTAMIA, ANSHAN, SYRIA, Seleucia, AKKAD, Susa, PERSIA, PHOENICIA, Palmyra, BAYLONIA, ELAM, CYPRUS, Sidon, Damascus, Baylon, SUMER, Lagash, Persepolis, INDIA, Tyre, Ur, Charax, Hormuz, PALESTINE, Jerusalem, Teredon, Spasina, GEDROSIA, Mediterranean Sea, Gaza, NABATAEA, Arabian Gulf, Alexandria, Pelusium, Petra, Memphis, Suez, Aqabah, THAMUD, Thaj, Muscat, MIDIAN, Tayma, Gerrha, BAHRAIN, Suhar, EGYPT, Madain Salih, Dedan, OMAN, Thebes, LIHYAN, Yathrib (Madinah), YAMAMAH, Yabrin, Arabian Sea, Layla, Jeddah, Quryat al-Faw, Rub Al - Khali, Calicut, Makkah, Dhufar, Nubia, Salalah, Nile, Mahrah, Hadhramaut, Red Sea, Shabwah, Marib, Mukalla, ETHIOPIA, Sana'a, QATABAN, HIMYAR, AWSAN, Aden

Legend
- Roman Empire
- Parthian Empire
- Fertile Crescent
- Nabataeans
- Palmyra
- Himyarites
- Sabaeans

0   1500 Km
0   1000 Miles

sufficiently horrifying for the event to be long remembered. Abraha was repelled. The people were mainly Jews and Christians, providing fertile soil for the Prophet's revelation. The region was also influenced by the Byzantines, (who supported their fellow-Christian Abyssinians) Syrians and Persians; influences which flowed in with traders following the ancient trade routes, pre-Islamic pilgrims visiting the Black Stone in Makkah and by poets making for the festival at Ukhaz. Arabic became established as the language of Arabia with the Qur'an. It had been the spoken language of the Nabataeans and north Arabians, although they wrote in Aramaic.

The picture of central Arabia in the early centuries AD is one of the increasing power of the nomadic groups, whose numbers were swelled about the third century AD by incursions from the south-west. At the same time settlements in the well-watered areas of the Wadi Hanifah, al-Kharj and Aflaj were growing in size. The Himyarites of Yemen and the Persian Sassanids tried to ensure that the rich trade from the south

passed safely through the central region. The Himyarites' method of gaining control was to form alliances with tribes, in particular the warlike tribe of Kindah. In the fifth and sixth centuries it was the Kindah who welded the tribes together and installed a semblance of unity and peace which enabled the settlements to thrive. Poems of the early sixth century AD paint a picture of peace and plentiful harvests in Yamamah. Trade flourished in this peaceful period and the settlements grew more powerful. After Makkah achieved sacred significance in the sixth century as a pre-Islamic sanctuary, Hajr (modern Riyadh) commanded the route to Makkah from the east (as it did later under Islam) and this gave it a strong position, enhanced by its dedication as a "sacred enclosure", one of several in pre-Islamic Arabia. The "false" prophet Musaylimah arose in Yamamah at much the same time as Muhammad in Makkah and for a time the central region opposed the introduction of Islam. They were brought to submission to Islam after the battle of Aqraba (in today's Palestine) in AD 634.

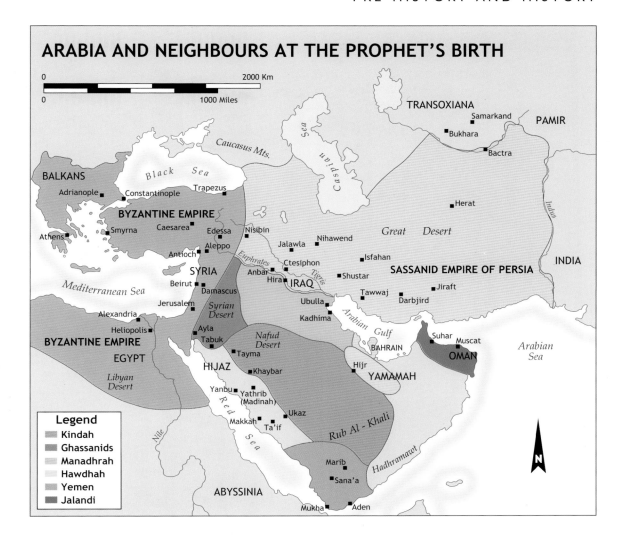

ARABIA AND NEIGHBOURS AT THE PROPHET'S BIRTH

Imru Al-Qays

Spoken Arabic poetry had already evolved into a refined art form by the time it was captured in written script around the period of the birth of Islam in the early seventh century AD. It thus 'arrived' intact, already perfectly formed, to provide the foundation of all future creative writing in Arabic.

The immeasurably ancient oral heritage of the Bedouin poets stemmed from the manner of their life. Disciplined by rhyme and metre, the medium flourished, expressing the hopes and fears of the wandering tribal communities. The themes were honour, love, prowess in battle, and resilience in the face of the constant threats posed by the fierce sun and the rugged terrain.

Foremost among these early poets stands Imru al-Qays, supreme master of the genre and widely credited as the inventor of the classical ode, the *qasidah*. Youngest son of Hujr, the last king of

Stop, let us weep, pause to weep over the
*   remembrance of my beloved,*
Here was her abode on the edge of the sandy desert
*   between Dakhool, Howmal, Tudiha and al-Miqrat.*
The traces of her encampment are not wholly
*   obliterated even now,*
For when the South wind blows the sand over them,
*   the North wind sweeps it away.*

Kindah, an ancient tribe from the South West of the peninsula, Imru al-Qays started composing poetry at an early age. The passionate eroticism of his poetry soon enraged his father, who banished him, and the young poet took to composing his verse while wandering as a vagabond in the desert. It was while he was thus wandering that his tribe went to war with the Bani Assad tribe, only to be destroyed, his fathered murdered. Imru al-Qays swore revenge and gathered a force to return the attack. Although he was successful in routing the Bani Assad, he spent much of the rest of his life unsuccessfully trying to raise further forces to destroy the them utterly.

Probably the most famous poem in the Arabic language is Imru al Qays' long eulogy to Unayzah *(inset here)*, which opens with the author pining over the remains of a deserted encampment, a scene which was to become the set piece opening for all other *qasidahs* of this genre.

Right:

The fort at Tarut, photographed in 1950, is presumed to have been built by the Portuguese in the 1520s.

Below right:

This Ottoman map, printed in Istanbul, 1732, was compiled after the Ottomans had relinquished their hold on al-Hasa. "Lahsa", Qatif and Bahrain are named.

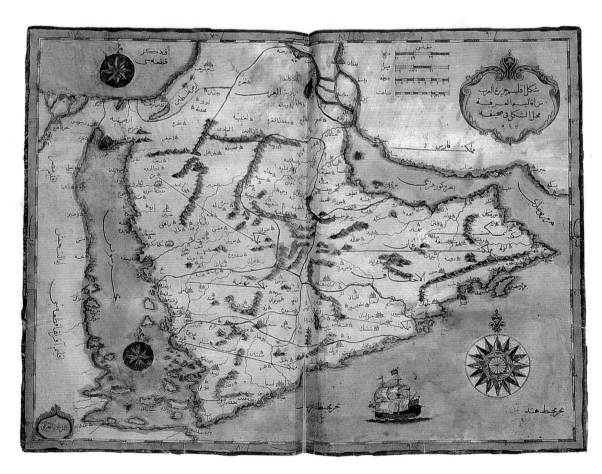

Arabia Under Islam

Makkah and Madinah, home of Islam and the early Caliphs, changed their character completely after the Caliphate moved to Damascus. Then, as Philip Hitti says, "The quiet life of Madinah, rendered venerable by its early Moslem association, attracted thither would-be scholars devoted to the study of the mementos of its sacred past and to the collecting of legal and ritual enactments." Those wishing to escape the turmoil of political and military activity elsewhere retired to Madinah and built great palaces. Pilgrims and others poured wealth into the holy cities which sent huge sums in tribute to the Caliphs.

Under the Abbasids the Hejaz became, with central Arabia (Yamamah), a province under a governor and continued to be the wealthiest part of Arabia. The Abbasids had an advanced postal system with a network of roads along which not only post but also pilgrims making for Makkah were able to travel. There were caravanserais, hospices and cisterns dotted along the main roads. In the Hejaz in the tenth century AD a descendant of the Prophet declared himself Sharif of Makkah, and the Sharifate thus founded survived, sometimes independently, sometimes under outside control, until Abdul Aziz Ibn Saud conquered the Hejaz in 1925.

The Eastern region was quick to adopt Islam. In Jawatha in the Al-Hasa Oasis stands the first mosque in Arabia outside Madinah. Its remains can still be seen. The Persians were expelled and the whole eastern seaboard of the Gulf became incorporated into a single Muslim province under Basra. Under the Abbasids, governors were appointed from Baghdad and a golden age of trade in the Gulf was ushered in.

By the ninth century Abbasid control was disintegrating, allowing the Qarmatians to take control. They ruled the region from their capital in al-Hasa, disrupting the pilgrimage and in AD 930 even capturing the Black Stone from the Ka'abah. Later they became more orthodox in their practice of Islam, returning the Black Stone to Makkah and having a rapprochement with the Abbasids. Thereafter

different groups took power in the region, the prize being control of trade in the Gulf. Persians operating from the island of Hormuz were able to impose stability on this trade for a while. However, by the sixteenth century the Portuguese and Ottomans were vying for control. The Ottomans can be said to have been the winners in this rivalry as they kept an intermittent hold on the region until finally expelled by Abdul Aziz Ibn Saud in 1913. But the mark that the Portuguese left can be seen in the Portuguese forts standing to this day on Bahrain, Tarut Island, Hormuz and Muscat.

The towns of central Arabia adopted Islam after the battle of Aqraba and enjoyed the peace and stability brought by strong central authority, exercised at first from Damascus and later from Baghdad. Riyadh, then called Hajr, was the administrative capital of the region under the Umayyads, and the Abbasids. Under the latter, large sums of tax were collected from the area, demonstrating the prosperity then being enjoyed.

From the ninth century, however, central power wielded from Baghdad weakened and the settlements were at the mercy of their nomadic tribal neighbours. However, as William Facey describes in his history of Riyadh, visiting travellers like the Persian Nasir-i-Khusraw who visited al-Kharj (then Yamamah) in the eleventh century, described the flowing streams and abundant date harvests of that area and Ibn Battutah in the fourteenth visited Riyadh (then Hajr) and reported on its streams and its trees.

In the fifteenth century the Jabris of al-Hasa, "renowned for their power, piety and respect for justice", as Facey says, controlled the towns of the Wadi Hanifah and al-Kharj and brought stability to the region. Climatically this was also a favourable time for the establishment of larger settlements in central Arabia. Several new towns arose in the fifteenth and sixteenth centuries. There was another shift in power in favour of settled people and their values. With the establishment of the town of Dir'iyyah in the Wadi Hanifah, the history of central Arabia becomes the rising power of the al-Saud, and is covered below.

Rabadah

From the earliest days of Islam, believers have made the pilgrim's journey to Makkah, the *Hajj*, gathering from all four corners of the world. The route was often hazardous, across capricious seas or harsh deserts. Probably most famous of the pilgrim routes is the Darb Zubaydah – Zubaydah's Road – named in memory of the wife of the Abbasid Caliph, Harun Al-Rashid. Lined with wells and hospices, the route runs from Mesopotamia, taking a southwesterly course across the desert and down to the fertile Hejaz, to arrive at Makkah, just east of the Red Sea port of Jeddah. The unpaved route is still identifiable after thirteen centuries, and was in use in recent memory.

The archaeology of the stopping posts along the pilgrim trail gives an insight into how the earliest pilgrims travelled and were catered for *en route*. The site of Rabadah, a former town about one third of the way on the return route, in the foothills of the Hejaz mountains, was investigated by an archaeological research team from King Saud University from 1979, and has been carefully excavated since. The finds demonstrate that there was once a thriving city here on the trail, with coins dating from the eighth century CE (an Abbasid dinar dating from AH 171 is shown *left*). Pottery and glasswork crafted locally, and stone artefacts (such as in the *centre picture*) created from materials extracted from the neighbouring steatite mine were also discovered.

Above:

The ruined fort at Dammam, shown here in 1934, possibly the one which served as a base for the notorious Rahman ibn Jabir until 1826.

Right:

Abd al-Wahhab's house in Dir'iyyah has been restored to its original condition.

Rise of Saudi Arabia

The Saudi state had its origins in Najd, central Arabia. The Saudi family traces its descent from Mani ibn Rabia al-Muraydi, who came in 1446 from al-Hasa to settle in Wadi Hanifah. By the beginning of the seventeenth century his descendants had established themselves as rulers of a small emirate centred on Dir'iyyah to the north of Riyadh. Shortly before 1720, Saud ibn Muhammad, the eponymous founder of the family, became ruler. He was succeeded, on his death in 1725, by his son Muhammad.

Wahhabism takes its name from Muhammad ibn Abd al-Wahhab, who was born in 1703 into a family of religious scholars at Uyaynah, the centre of another emirate in Wadi Hanifah, to the north of Dir'iyyah. He was brought up to follow the Hanbali Law School, the most rigorous of the four law schools of Sunni Islam, and from an early age was noted for his strictness. In the course of his education he became influenced by the ideas of Ibn Taymiyya, a theologian and jurist who died in 1328 and who had argued for a purification of Islam from what he considered to be accretions to the primitive faith. His ideas had some influence, especially among followers of the Hanbali Law School, and Ibn Abd al-Wahhab came to believe that the essential monotheism of Islam had been compromised by excessive veneration of the Prophet Muhammad and other "saints". This veneration was most commonly expressed in pilgrimages and visits to minor sanctuaries and to the tombs of holy men; so Ibn Abd al-Wahhab preached against these. He also insisted on the stricter implementation of penalties – such as death for adultery – fixed in the Qur'an, and he forbade certain innovations, notably the smoking of tobacco.

In 1745, after setbacks elsewhere, Ibn Abd al-Wahhab settled in Dir'iyyah, where he was favourably received by Muhammad ibn Saud. This event marks the beginning of a seventy-year period of expansion for the Dir'iyyah emirate, the first of three distinct phases in the history of the Saudi state. Modern Saudi Arabia is the product of the third of these phases. The religious ideology of the leaders appealed equally to the tribes and to the settled population – the latter provided the main support for the dynasty in the first two phases, and the tribes were crucial in the third.

By the end of the eighteenth century AD the emirate of Dir'iyyah had extended its authority over Najd, finally gaining control of Riyadh in 1773.

By 1792 when Ibn Abd al-Wahhab died, his ideas had already proved more directly influential than those of Ibn Taymiyya ever were. The rapid expansion of the Saudi emirate inevitably provoked fear and hostility in neighbouring non-Wahhabi states. The Sharif of Makkah undertook a series of expeditions against the Saudi state which now bordered his in the Hejaz, but these expeditions were unsuccessful, and in 1803 AD, shortly before the death of Abdul Aziz, who had succeeded his father Muhammad in 1765, a Saudi army brought Makkah under Saudi control. Two years later Madinah was taken. In the north the Ottoman governors of Iraq supported the anti-Wahhabi tribes on the border between Iraq and Arabia, but they too were unable to hold back the Wahhabi forces.

The Saudi occupation of the Hejaz brought the Saudi state into direct conflict with the Ottoman Sultan, who regarded himself as the guardian of the Holy Places for the whole Muslim world. At first the Sultan was unable to act, but in AD 1811 the Albanian, Muhammad Ali, having secured control of Egypt, organized, at the Sultan's command, an expedition against the Wahhabis.

In 1812 forces from Egypt, led by Muhammad Ali's son Tusun, took Madinah and in the following year Makkah. Saud, the son of Abdul Aziz, died in 1814, and his successor, his son Abdullah, had to conclude a truce with Tusun, ceding control of the Holy Cities to Muhammad Ali. In 1816, however, fighting began again, an army from Egypt invaded Najd, and in 1818 Dir'iyyah was taken. Abdullah was sent in captivity to Istanbul, where he was executed. This was the end of the First Saudi State.

In 1824 Turki, the son of Abdullah ibn Muhammad, seized Riyadh from Muhammad Ali's forces. From then until the last two decades of the nineteenth century, when the

Right:

Abdul-Rahman Al Saud, (1850-1928), the father of Abdul Aziz ibn Saud.

Saudi state was taken over by the Rashidi rulers of Ha'il in Jabal Shammar, Riyadh was the capital of the Second Saudi State. From there Turki extended his authority over the whole of Najd, inner Oman, and al-Hasa, which had been occupied for a time by Muhammad Ali's forces. Abdul Rahman ibn Hasan, a grandson of Ibn Abd al-Wahhab, was appointed by Turki to be *qadi* of Riyadh, and he, together with his son, Abd al-Latif, was largely responsible for the prevailing influence of Wahhabism in the nineteenth century.

In 1834 Turki was assassinated in a dispute between members of the Saudi family, but his son Faisal managed to wrest power from the rebels who had seized Riyadh. In the following year Faisal appointed Abdullah ibn Ali ibn Rashid to be his governor in Ha'il. Ibn Rashid's descendants were eventually to extend their power and establish their own rule over the Saudi state. Between 1838 and

1843 Faisal's rule in Riyadh was interrupted when Muhammad Ali again sent a force to invade Najd and set up another member of the Saudi family as ruler under the supervision of his agent in Riyadh. Faisal himself was taken prisoner to Cairo, but escaped and re-established his rule with the help of Abdullah ibn Rashid.

Faisal's death in 1865 was followed by a struggle for power between two of his sons, Abdullah and Saud, a conflict which enabled the Ottomans to win back al-Hasa and the ruler of Ha'il, Muhammad ibn Rashid, to extend his power over the Saudi state, while ostensibly seeking to uphold the rights of Abdullah. By the time of Abdullah's death in 1889, the Saudi state was no more than a province of the territory ruled by the Rashidis from Ha'il. Two years later Abdullah's brother and successor, Abdul Rahman, was expelled from Riyadh by Muhammad ibn Rashid who appointed a puppet governor of the walled city. Abdul Rahman and his family, including his young son Abdul Aziz, who had been born about 1880, fled to Kuwait, which was at this time an independent sheikhdom.

It was Abdul Aziz ibn Abdul Rahman, usually called simply Ibn Saud, who initiated the third phase in the history of the Saudi state, lasting from the beginning of the twentieth century AD until the present day. In 1902 he was able to take advantage of the weakness of Rashidi power, following the death of Muhammad ibn Rashid in 1897, by recapturing Riyadh with the help of what was really no more than a raiding party from Kuwait.

The following ten years were spent in ousting the Rashidis from Qasim and in inconclusive fighting against the tribes. It was not until 1912 that Ibn Saud took a step which was to prove decisive – the inauguration of the Ikhwan ("brethren") movement. During his exile in Kuwait and while fighting with the Rashidis, Abdul Aziz had come to see the military potential of the nomadic tribes if their customary resistance to state control could be overcome. He realized that he must settle the tribesmen and give them a motive for uniting, just as at the time of the Arab conquests in mediaeval times the

Travellers in Arabia

Carston Niebuhr (1733-1815), a German, leading a prevailingly Danish expedition arrived by sea in Jeddah in 1732, and proceeded to Mocha, in Yemen.

Johann Burckhardt (1784-1817), a Swiss, landed at Jeddah 1812, and between then and 1815 travelled to Makkah and Madinah.

Richard Burton's (1821-90) famous journey on the pilgrim route took place in 1853.

Lady Anne Blunt (1837-1917) was the first woman to cross the Nafud desert and visit Ha'il.

Charles Doughty (1843-1926) wrote his Travels in Arabia Deserta after journeys in the Hejaz and Najd.

Gertrude Bell (1868-1926), a fine Arabist and tribal expert, reached Ha'il in 1914.

T.E. Lawrence (1888-1935) is famous for his role in the Arab Revolt against the Ottomans during the First World War.

Harry St. John Philby (1885-1960) explored and mapped more widely than any other.

Wilfred Thesiger (1910-2003) made several journeys in the Rub al-Khali in the 1950s, after the pioneering crossing of the same desert by Bertram Thomas in 1931 from Saleh to Qatar.

The dangers of desert travel and Arab caution towards foreign intruders deterred Westerners until quite recently. In 1761 Carsten Niebuhr, a German in the service of Denmark, travelled in Western Arabia. So, too, did the Swiss J. L. Burkhardt in 1814. The British explorer Richard Burton, setting out in 1853, like Burkhardt followed the *hajj* route. Starting in Alexandria, he landed at Yanbu. Later he travelled in Midian.

At much the same time, another Englishman, Charles Doughty, was travelling in north-western and west central Arabia. First to enter the "cradle of the Arab race", as Lady Anne Blunt called the Najd, was the Finnish professor Wallin, reaching Ha'il in 1848. The Levantine Italian, Guarmani, started from Jerusalem in 1863, with a commission to buy horses, and reached Tayma, Buraydah, Ha'il and al-Jawf. The Jesuit missionary Palgrave travelled to Ha'il and Riyadh in 1862. The Blunts reached Ha'il in 1879. Captain Shakespear, a young assistant to the British Political Resident in Kuwait, brought the first motor car to Arabia and was the first Westerner to meet Ibn Saud, who later

described him as the greatest Westerner he had ever met. He was invited by Ibn Saud to come to Riyadh: this he combined with an epic journey across Arabia in 1914. While his life was short (he was killed in the battle of Jarab in 1915, wearing European clothes, a pith helmet and standing on a ridge to take photographs of the battle) his name continues to be revered in Arabia and he bequeathed a remarkable collection of photographs of the early Saudi state, including the standard-waving army of Ibn Saud on the march.

Of all the subsequent outstanding travellers in Arabia – Alois Musil, T. E. Lawrence, Gerard Leachman, Bertram Thomas, Wilfred Thesiger among others – none covered half as much territory as St John Philby. Setting off in 1917, he crossed Arabia from Uqayr in the east to Jeddah, travelling the following year through the Aflaj to Sulayyil. From then on he travelled extensively, journeying through the Rub al-Khali in 1932 and south from the Tihama to Mukalla in Hadhramaut in 1936. His last journeys in the early 1950s took him north through Wajh and Tabuk.

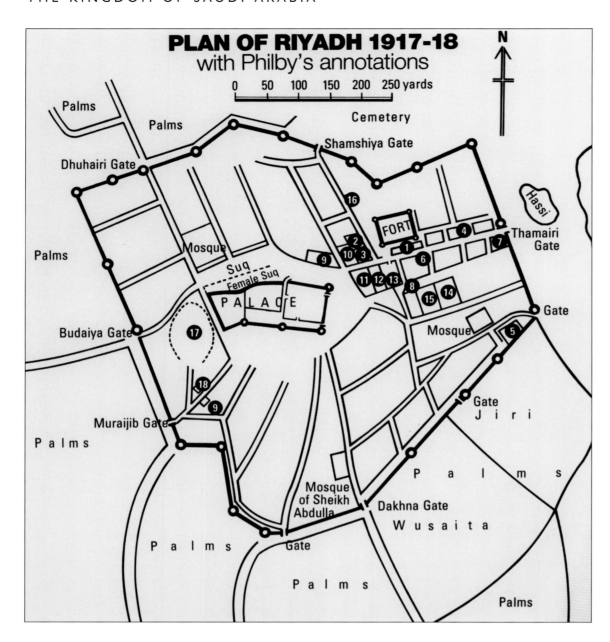

PLAN OF RIYADH 1917-18
with Philby's annotations

0 50 100 150 200 250 yards

N

Palms
Palms
Dhuhairi Gate
Cemetery
Shamshiya Gate
Palms
Mosque
Hassi
FORT
Thamairi Gate
Palms
Suq
Female Suq
PALACE
Budaiya Gate
Gate
Mosque
Muraijib Gate
Gate
Jiri
Palms
Palms
Mosque of Sheikh Abdulla
Dakhna Gate
Wusaita
Gate
Palms
Palms
Palms

1. *Mesjid al Qasr*
2. *Beit Ajnan*
3. *Old Palace*
4. *Abdullah Qusaiba*
5. *Mohammed's Stable*
6. *School*
7. *New Well*
8. *Shalhub*
9. *Saad*
10. *Turki*
11. *Mohammed*
12. *Abdulla*
13. *Imam*
14. *Faisal ibn Rashid*
15. *Saud*
16. *Junaifi*
17. *Baraha Muraijib*
18. *Ibrahim*

Musmak Fort today. Harry St John Philby reports that, following its capture in 1902, the Musmak Fort (left) fell on hard times, neglected and used as an arsenal and general storage space. Today, the restored building serves as a museum.

*The door of the Musmak Fort (**above right**) entered legend for the embedded spearhead, undisturbed from Ibn Saud's assault on the citadel in 1902. Ruling from the fort itself (**opposite**), Ibn Saud established security in the city and helped it to grow far beyond the original city walls (shown in Philby's map, **opposite, top**), with townspeople feeling confident to build dwellings beyond the enclosure's protection, illustrated in the aerial photograph of 1950 (**above**).*

tribesmen were abandoning their nomadic way of life for the garrison towns of the conquered territories. The first *hijrah* (military encampment) was founded at Artawiyyah in 1912. No record remains of the exact number of *hijrahs* established, but it was some two hundred or more, with between 10 and 10,000 warriors in each. With the help of the Ikhwan, Ibn Saud took Ha'il in 1921 and the whole of the Hejaz including Makkah, in 1924-26. Any further expansion in Arabia or its border areas would entail a clash with Great Britain, which was involved as protector or mandatory power in all of the territories except Yemen now bordering the Saudi state. The Ikhwan began to act more independently. In 1929 they attacked a party of Najdi merchants, and the revulsion which this act aroused among the settled population of the

Najd, as well as among several of the tribes, strengthened Ibn Saud's hand sufficiently for him to take action against the Ikhwan.

Early in 1930 a number of the Ikhwan's leaders surrendered to the British authorities in Kuwait, whence they were extradited by Ibn Saud. He spared their lives but imprisoned them in Riyadh.

This marked the end of the power of the Ikhwan as a force independent of Ibn Saud. Some of their *hijrahs* continued to exist, but were now under government control. Eventually the Ikhwan were incorporated in the National Guard. After 1930 Ibn Saud began the transformation of the state which is still continuing. The battle of Sabalah marked the end of the era in which the history of Saudi Arabia can be evaluated only in terms of the historical heritage.

59

Ibn Saud (Abdul Aziz ibn Saud), his brothers and his elder sons at camp near Thaj are seen here photographed by Captain William Shakespear in March 1911. In this photograph, Ibn Saud is seated, centre, with, standing behind him on the left, wearing two long plaits, his brother Sa'd ibn Abdul Rahman, who was killed at Kinzan just four years later, in 1915.

From Abdul Aziz to the Present Day

Saudi Arabia's stability owes much to the fact that a single dynasty has governed it since Abdul Aziz ibn Saud formally established the Kingdom in 1932. Abdul Aziz ibn Saud, is remembered by all who knew him for characteristics which distinguished him among the Arabs of his generation. Physically, he was outstandingly tall; self-disciplined to be hardy, he relished battle and was indifferent to injury. Spiritually, his faith dominated his life; he was deeply devout, and steadfast in upholding the puritanism preached to his forbears by the eighteenth century Islamic reformer, Ibn Abdul al-Wahhab. Mentally, he was a master of politics; his appraisal of men and their capacities was shrewd, and his grasp of world affairs astounding in one who during his long life paid only three brief visits outside his native Arabia, and never left the Arab world. Lastly, his basic instincts – integrity, a sense of honour, of justice, of humour – added up to

a nature that brought him success despite early vicissitudes in his chequered life.

He was born in or about 1880 and, as described above, at the age of 21 he left his family in Kuwait and, taking advantage of some leisurely skirmishing between Kuwaitis and Rashidis, slipped inland with 40 picked companions. In a night of surprises and sharp sword thrusts, he recaptured his family's home town, Riyadh. In 1902 his father, glad to reward determination allied to piety, named him Emir of Najd and Imam of its puritanical brand of Islam.

By 1926 he had captured the Holy Cities of Makkah and Madinah and the whole Red Sea coastal province of the Hejaz. He declared himself King of the Hejaz and Najd, and in 1932 renamed his kingdom Saudi Arabia. The use he made of the Ikhwan brotherhood has been described above. He gradually introduced the innovations he knew would be seen by the Saudi people as heresies, such as the telephone, pilgrimage by motor transport and wireless telegraphy.

Yet it was in his dealings with great powers that he best showed his acumen, and

awareness of Arab limitations which made him an outstanding diplomat. For instance, though he hated the two Hashemite fellow-Arabians whom the British had installed as rulers in neighbouring Iraq and Transjordan, he punished tribal or religious forays into their territory. Again in 1934 when armies led by his sons were on the verge of conquering Yemen, to their chagrin he ordered them to withdraw, because he realized that their approach to the borders of Aden and the coast of Eritrea was antagonizing both Britain and Italy. He was always friendly, though circumspect, with the British, surrounded as he was by their sea power, their mandates and their dependencies. Even during the darkest days of the Second World War, he warned them of potential misjudgments and hostility and backed them to win in the end. Only on the subject of Palestine did he censure them, then and later. As he listened, conscious of Arab impotence, to broadcasts about the British handling of Palestine's dismemberment, tears, it is said, poured down his cheeks.

At home, the greatest boon that he gave his people was internal security. Until his reign, all towns were walled, all gates barred at nightfall, all desert journeys undertaken at risk from raiders or feuding tribes. At the sight of strangers, friend could be told from foe only by some conventional gesture such as waving a headcloth or throwing up sand; if no such sign were given, the safest course was to gallop out of sight. Ibn Saud put an end to these hazards. His ways of doing so were to appoint trusted Najdis as regional governors, usually members of his vast family or of related stock – the Sudairis, Jiluwis or Thunayyans: these outposts he furnished with the mobile wireless trucks that enabled him to keep a watch – miraculous to the tribes – on desert behaviour. He also travelled widely and frequently among them, often cementing loyalties as he went by arranging a marriage between some sheikhly family and his own. By the time of his death, town walls were a thing of the past; he had induced the Ikhwan survivors to settle in agricultural colonies, and a traveller could stop and pray at the lawful hour or camp at nightfall

without fear of molestation, as he can today.

When Ibn Saud won his kingdom, it was pitifully poor. It produced only the bare necessities of life; its so-called roads were tracks; its ports were mere anchorages; its sole source of foreign exchange was pilgrimage dues. Religious learning apart, education was scanty; he had to resort to foreign Arabs as his advisers. All but one of his immediate entourage were literally advisers, for though he listened to information, he took all decisions, however trivial, himself. The exception was the one Najdi among them – his Minister of Finance, Abdullah Sulaiman. Ibn Saud, though the equal of anyone in political skill, negotiation or paternalistic power of decision, hated administration and was not good at it. As the business of his kingdom swelled and paperwork piled up, he was fortunate in having at his elbow for over twenty years one Najdi possessed of executive flair.

When the outbreak of the world economic crisis of the early 1930s seriously reduced the numbers making the pilgrimage, the repercussions magnified beyond management his kingdom's endemic poverty. At this

The Ruwala tribe of northern Arabia on the move – in 1926. Their tribal standard, seen here, was called the Markab, *the 'ship'. A frame of acacia wood like a large litter, it was decorated with black ostrich feathers. It was said that for centuries past it had moved from tribe to tribe, as one conquered the other, and that the Ruwala had kept it since about 1775. In time of battle a chosen Ruwala maiden would be carried in it exhorting her warriors who would defend her till their last breath – an echo of mediaeval chivalry.*

moment of crisis, a stroke of fortune relieved his plight. In 1932, oil was discovered in Bahrain, an island visible from the Saudi mainland. Mining geologists suspected that oil deposits might underlie the mainland also. An American oil company, offering to pay gold for prospection rights, enabled the desperate King and Finance Minister to round a tight corner. So began the exploration and discovery that, once the Second World War was over, turned Saudi Arabia's oil production into the most promising and wealthiest venture in an oil-rich peninsula.

Ibn Saud was abstemious throughout his life. His tastes were simple. Prayer and reading the scriptures took up many hours of each day; late in life he composed his own anthology of religious wisdom, sayings and proverbs. He rejoiced in family life; children and grandchildren were his delight; a cluster of them surrounds him in every informal photograph. Since at his death he left behind him forty-seven living sons (the youngest under seven) and unnumbered daughters, children were always in plentiful supply. He could be irascible, but not

for long. Among his greatest pleasures were desert life and pursuits, camping for part of every year, hunting, hawking, tests of horsemanship, camel racing. Whether in tent or palace, his mornings were spent giving audience in a *majlis* open to all his subjects, hearing grievances, righting wrongs, dispensing reward and punishment. Duty done, he liked to spend his afternoons in the peace of the desert, on some restive horse when in his prime, travelling by car in old age. A tremendous talker, his evenings were spent in discourse; topics on which he liked to dwell were theological niceties, such as the distinction between pure and impure belief; desert genealogies, which he had at his fingertips, and the details of old campaigns. He was a devout man who consistently relished the gift of life. Legend and anecdote sometimes tell more of a man's character than a recital of fact. It is said that when he captured Ha'il in 1921, a traitorous defender let him into the town by one of its five gates; he honoured the captains of the other four and punished the traitor. He handed out judgement with assurance and long remembered imaginativeness – summary execution for a

Ibn Saud rose to power primarily as a warrior, but it was only due to his diplomacy and statesmanship skills that he was able to carve a nation out of the people of such a vast and disparate territory, and to establish far-reaching diplomatic links for the fledging state.

*Seen above is Ibn Saud with King Farouk of Egypt (**top picture**), Winston Churchill, Prime Minister of Britain (**left**) and President Roosevelt of the USA (**right**), all of whom met him in Egypt in February 1945. An official portrait of the King in later life (**opposite**) shows him seated in the comfortable surroundings of the Murabba Palace, Riyadh.*

*This official portrait of King Abdul Aziz (Ibn Saud) shows him seated in front of the two sons who were to succeed him on the throne after his death, as King Saud (**right**) and King Faisal (**left**).*

villain, coupled with compassion for the victims of his crime, the shaving off of the beard and moustache of a young man who had simply been pert. Until crippled by arthritis, he liked to join in fun or horseplay; part of his personal success with his subjects was the spontaneity with which he rubbed shoulders with a crowd or joined in a war-dance. He loved an apt quip. St John Philby, often described as his "British adviser", was never this, but rather his walking encyclopaedia and verbal sparring-partner.

The Second World War changed the status and outlook of most Arab lands. They joined forces in a League; they gained admission to the United Nations; they gave new forms of expression to their nationalism. Some began to earn income from the oil that had been discovered before the war; most planned to use this new wealth for development and welfare. Looking back, it is odd to remember that, at this stage, the states which made all the running in the Arab League were Egypt, Iraq and Syria; Saudi Arabia's contribution to the League's budget was seven per cent of the total as against Egypt's forty-two per cent.

Only from 1950, when it made its "fifty-fifty" arrangement with the Arabian-American Oil Company (Aramco), did Saudi Arabia throw off its image of barren desert, backward inhabitants and poverty. By 1950, in which year Petromin and Aramco recorded that oil production topped twenty-five million tons, the King's health had deteriorated. An old eye trouble worsened; old wounds generated arthritis; unwillingly, he took to a wheelchair; inch by inch he lost his grip as he fought a long last illness. He grew unequal to controlling leaks of revenue. He had named his son Saud as Crown Prince. He died in 1953.

The House of Saud

1 From whom the Jiluwi branch of the
  House of Saud derive their name.
2 From whom the Abdullah-al-Turki branch
  of the House of Saud derive their name.
3 Known as "al Kabir", a name retained
  by his descendants.

FAHD The Seven Sons of King Abdul Aziz by the late Hassa
  bint Sudairi, who are known as the Al Fahd

Note: This family tree, though the result of meticulous research,
does not attempt to be comprehensive.
Source: King Abdul Aziz Archive.

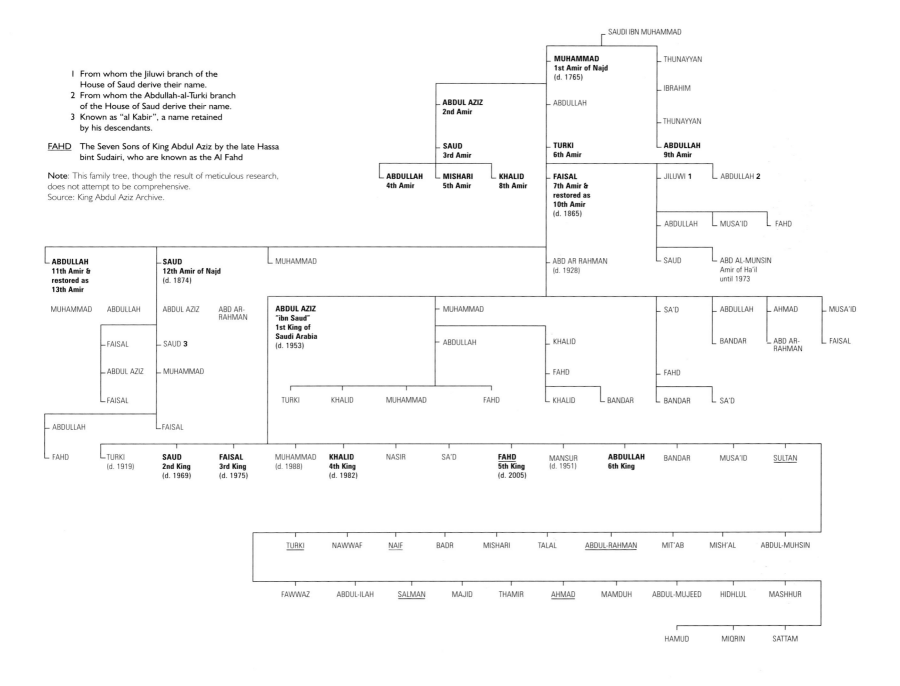

King Saud (1953-1964)

Saud, eldest surviving son of King Abdul Aziz (Ibn Saud), was born the day his father took Riyadh in 1902. In 1926 he was named Viceroy of Najd and in 1933 was designated Crown Prince some 20 years before his father died. He succeeded his father in 1953 at a difficult time in the Middle East. It was characterised by a fashionable republicanism and wild radio propaganda from abroad. Nasser was the new hero of the market place. The sudden influx of wealth in Saudi Arabia found the country without an infrastructure to cope with its opportunities. King Saud made an effort to remedy that situation by spending on hospitals, schools and road building. He was popular with the people and courteous, genial and generous to those around him. Owing to his ill health, however, he was not able to keep as firm a control over state expenditure and the budget as was felt necessary for the good of the country. He was, with the consensus of the al-Saud family, replaced as head of Government by his brother, Crown Prince Faisal, in 1958. Faisal succeeded almost immediately in balancing the budget and restoring the economy, which had been on the brink of bankruptcy. In 1964 Saud abdicated and Faisal became king.

*King Saud was the eldest of Ibn Saud's sons, his right-hand man and immediate successor to the throne, shown here as a young man in 1928 (**left**) and as monarch, with President John F. Kennedy of the United States of America in 1962 (**right**).*

King Faisal (1964-1975)

Faisal, born in 1906, just four years after his father had won back the Kingdom, was known for his piety and integrity. In 1919 his father's new friends the British offered a member of his family a trip to England as a reward for services in the First World War. The King chose Faisal for the treat and Faisal justified the choice. With the dignity that was to mark him throughout his career, he exchanged swords with King George V and, in the freezing cold of a post-war December, gravely accepted the visits that were thought suitable to his years – to the Zoo, to the Greenwich telescope and to the musical *Choo Chin Chow*. By 1925-1926, when his father overpowered the Sharifian family and conquered the Holy Cities of Makkah and Madinah, he was thought old enough to command an army. He brought up the reinforcements for which his father sent in order to capture the sea port of Jeddah. Later he was to prove his military capabilities more conclusively by commanding the most successful of the armies used by his father on the last of his campaigns – that of 1934 – by means of which he settled his frontier with the Yemen. Faisal's army, which sped down the coastal plain of the Red Sea, was the spearhead of this operation.

For all his success in the field, it was in the council chamber that Faisal's talents showed up best. Makkah and Jeddah once conquered, Ibn Saud proclaimed himself King of the Hejaz and Najd; but he could not be everywhere at once and he appointed Faisal his Viceroy in the Hejaz, with his seat in Makkah. Faisal received visitors in his father's absence and was his father's deputy in many dealings with non-Islamic states. In 1926, he was sent to Europe to broaden his outlook in Britain and France, and five years later he embarked on a wide-ranging tour that included Soviet Russia. (Saudi-Soviet relations at the time were good, for Soviet Russia, with its own Muslims in mind, had been one of the first foreign states to recognize the new King and his Kingdom.)

Ibn Saud throughout his life continued personally to handle dealings with foreigners

if they came to Arabia for instance, to negotiate frontiers or seek concessions, but abroad he left everything to Faisal, whom he appointed as his Foreign Minister. Faisal, who during the Second World War had further enlarged his experience of the world by visiting the United States with his brother Khalid (later King Khalid), became a figure of note in world conclaves. His father, smitten from 1950 with the illness of which he died in 1953, became wholly dependent on the two eldest of his 35 surviving sons – Saud, the Crown Prince, who had inherited touches of Ibn Saud's humour and gaiety, and Faisal, who was more like him in his piety and austerity, and in his understanding of human foibles.

*The young Faisal (aged 14 **above** and **opposite**, at prayer) assumed responsibility early, and was commanding an army by the age of 21. He came to be recognised as an international statesman and to be known for his austerity and piety.*

When the old King died and Saud succeeded him, the younger, graver brother became Prime Minister as well as Foreign Minister. At the time, Saudi Arabia lacked the institutions and the administrative framework that were becoming necessary if it was to handle its mounting revenue and fulfil its potential role in Arab affairs. Faisal responded to the challenge and, with the assistance of a devout and cautious Pakistani financier, set up the Saudi Arabian Monetary Agency (SAMA). In 1964 Crown Prince Faisal became King of Saudi Arabia. The role was not easy. To the right of him, the *ulema* and the more pious members of his family were pressing for a return to the austerity of his father's day; to his left, and in the forces, young men who had been abroad urged "modernization" and less rigorous adherence to the strict rules of religious extremists. Faisal, as was his wont, steered towards compromise. He permitted

television but not the cinema; he promoted secular and technical education for boys, but kept girls' education under the jurisdiction of the Sheikh al-Islam – the chief religious authority – while permitting his wife, Iffat, to develop Jeddah's Dar al-Hanan Educational Institute for girls as a beacon of modern education to secondary level.

His middle way was not everywhere popular. Whatever his personal inclinations (and he cannot have enjoyed the glare of lighting for the television cameras that he permitted even during audiences) he never forgot that it was the *ulema* who had helped him to restore the Kingdom to its proper course. Foreign policy, too, presented its problems. Nasser's Egypt, the most powerful of his neighbours, had to his consternation taken up arms in support of the republicans against the royalists in Yemen; Aden, which the British were about to leave, was a hotbed of left-wing

*From early on, King Abdul Aziz gave Faisal responsibility for foreign travel and much of foreign affairs policy. As King, Faisal travelled extensively. He is shown **above** on a state visit to London in May 1967, accompanied in the royal carriage by the sovereign's Lord-in-Waiting.*

*King Faisal was known as a devout man. He is shown **opposite (right)** wearing* ihram, *accompanied by his brothers Fahd (**centre**) and Abdullah (**left**).*

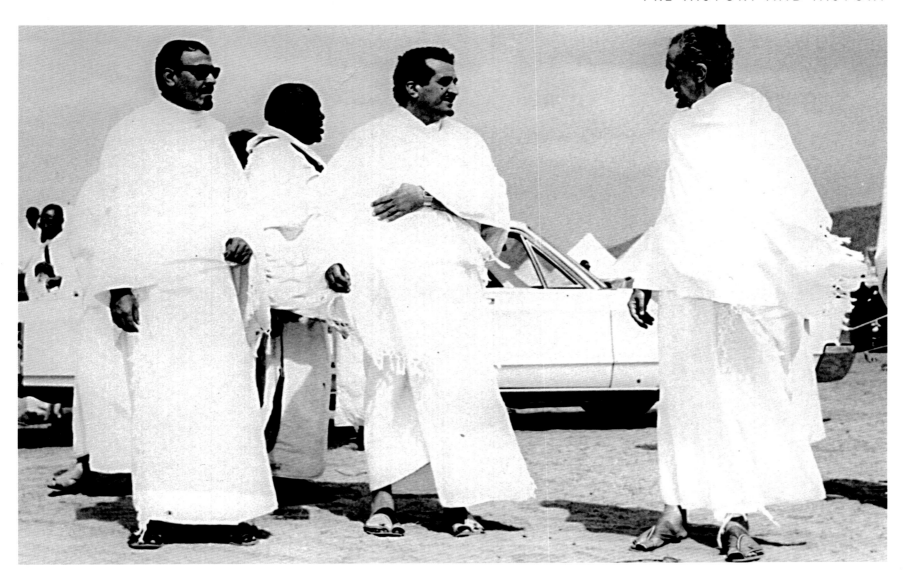

parties fanned by Egyptian propaganda; Syria and a newly-republican Iraq were flirting with his bugbear, Soviet Russia. He sought to create for himself a new base by visiting Islamic countries and establishing an Islamic summit that would include Iran and Pakistan. But this plan foundered because the Islamic states had differing political priorities. It won him little beyond the respect he already commanded as Defender of the Faith and guardian of its Holy Places.

The Palestine War of 1967 abruptly changed his role in foreign affairs. Egypt, till then a rival, was humiliated and truncated. So was Jordan. Jerusalem, the third holiest city of Islam, fell into Israel's hands. Faisal set about providing financial support for the states on Israel's borders. Nasser's death in 1970, and the passing of Egypt's presidency to a less dominant figure, Anwar Sadat, opened Faisal's way to the leading role in Arab affairs which, with his usual

dignity, he now assumed. Though in his late sixties and often far from well, he made long journeys to Arab summits in order to have his say. To him Zionism and Communism were twin evils, and he warmly approved when, in the summer of 1972, Sadat dismissed his Soviet advisers. Now nothing stood in the way of the full-blooded alliance that was capable of dominating the Arab scene – the marriage of Saudi wealth with Egyptian manpower and technical superiority. In July 1973 King Faisal gave the world an idea of what was in his mind when for the first time he publicly mentioned his country's power to cut back oil deliveries if President Nixon did not modify his support for Israel. The Arab oil embargo that accompanied the general oil price-rise during the October War of 1973 was applied only with his customary caution, but the effect was dramatic.

At the time of Faisal's death, his country was one of the richest in the world in liquid funds.

Riyadh, 70 years earlier a mud town, was a city throbbing with activity, besieged by salesmen and technical experts out for contracts to fulfil the developments he had in mind, pierced by dual carriageways, humming with traffic, twinkling at night with the lights that outline mile on mile of ribbon development, yet with *suqs* that fall quiet, empty of their menfolk, at the hour of prayer. Saudi Arabia's government was highly centralized, and King Faisal personally took most of the important decisions.

On the Prophet's birthday, 1975, one of his scores of nephews, the son of a much younger half brother, slipped into his audience chamber and fired three shots at the King over the shoulder of the Kuwaiti Oil Minister whom the King was receiving. Although the assassin's motives may never be completely understood, what is certain is that he acted to deprive his countrymen of a leader with a store of wisdom and experience.

King Khalid (1975-1982)

The stability of the Kingdom stood the test of this capricious act. King Khalid, next in line, moved naturally into the role of leader of the nation. His own wide experience and the talents of the immediate family – exemplified by Prince Fahd, the Crown Prince as First Deputy Prime Minister, and Prince Abdullah, the Second Deputy Prime Minister and Head of the National Guard – ensured the smooth continuance of government. Within six months, King Khalid launched the monumental Second Plan. Like his father, Khalid honoured the essentially Arabian quality of his roots. He was at home in the desert and trusted by the tribes. With his father he took part in several expeditions during the unification of the country. In 1932 he was appointed Governor of the Hejaz, and in 1934 Minister of the Interior. As a young man he represented the Kingdom on various missions abroad with his brother Faisal (e.g. to Britain in 1939 and 1945, and the US in 1943). As Faisal's First Deputy Prime Minister he moved to the centre of the affairs of state, was party to all major decisions of policy and frequently travelled abroad.

When he became King in 1975, Saudi Arabia was already committed to carefully planned development on a massive scale. Fahd was by his side as First Deputy Premier, dynamic and involved in the day-to-day administration of government. Khalid's heart disease, twice alleviated by open heart surgery, precluded sustained strenuous public duties. Yet it was remarkable what he achieved, repeatedly travelling at home and overseas in his kingly role, and playing a vital personal part in Arab and Islamic affairs. Khalid's intervention halted – for a while – the Lebanese civil war in the late 1970s; he also brought Muslims together in the historic 38-nation summit in Ta'if and Makkah in 1981, and that year launched the six-nation Gulf Cooperation Council.

He was a man of generosity of heart and personal modesty, offering warmth and sympathy to the most humble of supplicants. He had little time for the panoply of power. When he died in Ta'if on June 13, 1982, at the height of Israeli aggression in Lebanon, his people mourned a wise, fatherly and devoted leader.

King Fahd (1982-2005)

King Fahd, King Khalid's successor, was born in 1923. He was the eldest of the "Sudairi Seven", the seven sons of King Abdulaziz by Hussah bint Ahmad Al Sudairi, the favourite among the late King's many wives.

He was born as his father consolidated power on the Arabian Peninsula, taking control of Makkah and Madinah. At the age of nine years old the young Fahd watched as his father officially founded the Kingdom of Saudi Arabia by signing the treaty of Jeddah.

King Fahd travelled widely from an early age. In 1945 he made his first state visit, flying to New York City to attend the opening session of the General Assembly of the United Nations. In 1953, at the age of 30, he was appointed Education Minister by his father, and went on to establish the first expansion of schools across the Kingdom. In the same year he attended the coronation of Queen Elizabeth II on a state visit on behalf

of the House of Saud.

In 1962 he became Minister of the Interior, and in 1967, Second Deputy Prime Minister. When King Faisal was assassinated in 1975, King Khalid ascended to the throne, with Fahd succeeding as Crown Prince and First Deputy Prime Minister.. He acted as viceroy during King Khalid's absences, and remained at the heart of the daily affairs of stage throughout his brother's reign.

He came to power as a statesman known and respected on the international scene as a man of experience and consistency of policy, above all of restraint, caution and patience. These policies came into play throughout the continuing crises surrounding Israel and its neighbours, and Iraq, over which it was necessary for Saudi Arabia's alignment with the US over the restoration of Kuwait's sovereignty in the early 1990s to be replaced with a withdrawal of support for the US in its championship of the invasion of Iraq some years later. He consistently ensured that Saudi

*King Khalid (on the left, **opposite**, with his brother Fahd) maintained the momentum of the nation's development initiated by his predecessor, although burdened by ill health.*

*King Fahd, pictured at ease (**above**), supported his brother Khalid throughout his reign before succeeding him as King on his death in 1982.*

Arabia's economic authority, exercised thorugh OPEC and OAPEC, be directed towards maintaining stability in international pricing of oil.

He is also remembered for his generous foreign aid programme. Some 5.5 per cent of Saudi Arabia's national oil income was given, predominantly through the Saudi Fund for Development and the Opec Development Fund, to support causes internationally. King Fahd was active in a campaign to support the Bosnian Muslims in the Balkan wars.

Domestically, King Fahd was always intent on building a Saudi Arabia whose prosperity would endure, achieved by means of painstaking planning, sound education, diversification of the economy, conservation of resources, and devotion to Islam. Economically, the Kingdom faced troubled times in the early 1990s, facing the twin challenges of population growth and the drop in oil revenues. When the price of Saudi crude fell as low as $12 a barrel in January

1994, the government was forced to announce a 20 per cent reduction in public spending, an exigency that was to delay a number of the planned development projects. It was this exigency that was to necessitate reform of government, and in 1995 King Fahd replaced more than half of his 28 ministers with younger figures, a move which resulted in an improvement of the economic situation.

King Fahd's legacy will be seen, above all else, as the development of the national infrastructure – notably the schools, hospitals and roads. He will also be remembered for his attention to the evolution of representative or elected structures of government, notably at the municipal level but also in respect of reform of the constitution and the establishment of the Majlis as-Shura. Following his stroke in 1995, relative incapacity obliged the King to pass the everyday control of affairs to his heir apparent and brother, Crown Prince Abdullah.

King Abdullah

Abdullah bin Abdul Aziz succeeded his brother King Fahd as King of Saudi Arabia on the latter's death, and was formally enthroned on August 3, 2005.

King Abdul Abdul Aziz once said, "I train my own children to walk barefoot, to rise two hours before dawn, to eat but little, to ride horses bareback." More than any of Abdul Aziz's other sons, Abdullah exemplifies this prescription for bringing up children.

He was born in 1924, to King Abdul Aziz's eighth wife, Fahda bint Asi Al Shuraim, of the Shammar tribe. He was educated at the Royal Court in the elite Princes' School in Riyadh. He also spent much of his early life with the Bedouin out in the desert, and a love of this desert life, of falconry and equestrianism, and a respect for the traditional Bedouin values of honour, generosity, simplicity and courage, has remained with him.

*The King performing the traditional ardah sword dance (**opposite, left**).*

*King Abdullah (**opposite, far left**) had long supported his brother, King Fahd, before coming to the throne in August 2005. During this period he established a reputation for political integrity and for energetically pursuing a solution to the Palestinian conflict.*

Appointed head of the National Guard by King Faisal in 1962, he has long commanded the intense loyalty of the tribal battalions. While maintaining charge over the National Guard, he was appointed Second Deputy Prime Minister on the succession of King Khalid in 1975, and when King Fahd succeeded as monarch in 1982, he was named Crown Prince and First Deputy Prime Minister. In the latter capacity, he presided over cabinet meetings and governed the country as Deputy to the Custodian of the Two Holy Mosques, King Fahd bin Abdulaziz.

As Crown Prince, Abdullah's state visits overseas include France in 2005, Austria in 2004, Russia in 2003, and Germany in 2001, in addition to travels within the Arab and Islamic worlds.

In 2000, following the United Nations Millennium Summit in New York, he travelled to Brazil, Argentina, and Venezuela; and in 1998, in a world tour that included the United States, he visited Britain, France, China, Japan, South Korea and Pakistan.

Over the course of his many years supporting his brothers in running the country, he has always taken a keen interest in foreign policy issues, especially Saudi Arabia's relations with Arab and other Islamic countries, and Saudi Arabia's efforts to resolve various international crises, including the Lebanese civil war and the "Middle East peace process". It was Abdullah who, in March 2002, put forward the acclaimed Arab Peace Initiative in an attempt to resolve the Palestine problem. Published on the occasion of the Arab Summit in Beirut, it received the unanimous backing of the Arab states and focused international attention on the situation in the occupied territories.

King Abdullah is known for his piety and devotion to the Arab cause. A former US Ambassador described him as "a good Muslim, and incorrupt". He is also convinced of the importance of maintaining the country's traditions and respecting the cultural heritage. He oversees the annual festival of heritage at Janadriyah.

Crown Prince Sultan bin Abdulaziz

Crown Prince Sultan of Saudi Arabia, as with earlier Crown Princes, holds also the position of First Deputy Prime Minister. He was born in 1928, in Riyadh. Along with his brothers he received his early education in religion, culture and diplomacy at the royal court. He was appointed Governor of Riyadh in 1947. He became Minister of Agriculture in 1953 and Minister of Communications in 1955. It was during this period that he oversaw the construction of the Kingdom's rail link between Damam and Riyadh, as well as the building of road and other transport links. Crown Prince Sultan has been Minister of Defence and Aviation since 1962. In this formidable role he has presided over the astonishing expansion of Saudi Arabia's army, airforce and navy, ensuring that the Kingdom is defended by highly trained, and fully manned and well equipped defence forces.

3

Cultural Heritage

What men recite and sing, what they forge and fashion, have been inspired by the voices of poets, the Holy Qur'an and by the demands and joys of life in the desert and oasis. Yet the cities have seldom lacked an infusion of ideas and skills from the wider world.

By contrast, alongside all that which the term "arts and crafts" embraces, the modern buildings of today's Saudi Arabia illustrate the influence of traditional Arabian design on contemporary architecture designed by cosmopolitan practitioners.

The desert truffles, shown here in a picnic setting, are a rare and seasonal delicacy to be consumed fresh, with Arabian coffee.

Traditional Culture

The truest culture of Arabia rests not in things but in words, in the language. This is not only because in the nomadic life a man can possess no more than he and his camel can carry, but because the Holy Book, the Qur'an, is the fount of his culture as it is of his faith, and the verbal richness of the Qur'an is without parallel. As Islam became established throughout Arabia, the followers of the Prophet drew on the heritage of Arab tribal thought. Adherence to the Holy Law constituted the primary act of faith.

The absence of a priesthood meant that no clear distinction arose between the religious and the secular. No part of a man's daily life, or his thought, or his culture, lay outside his religion. The religious scholars who chronicled the early centuries of Islam incorporated in their works the sagas and genealogies of tribal life as well as the career of the Prophet and the Community of the Faithful. The traditions they recorded became precedents for the legal and social fabric of Islam. This body of writing emphasizes the significance of human lives and human acts. It contributed to the forming of a self aware Islamic culture in the Land of the Prophet. For its part, the Holy Qur'an itself, in its style, not only took into consideration the poetic traditions of the Bedouin, but also challenged their literary talent. Before the appearance of the Holy Book, the Bedouin had no written code of law, and only the custom of the blood vendetta ensured the protection of a man's life. Leaders had to rely on their own merits for their authority: it was necessary for such men to demonstrate the qualities which entitled them to their position.

The spare nomadic life of the Bedouin offered little chance for the development of the material arts. Only those forms which could survive the harsh demands of their existence

Amid the older generation, correct apparel involved the wearing of a ceremonial weapon, until late in the twentieth century.

Weaponry

Skilled smiths plied their trade in every permanent settlement. Yet the development of intricate workmanship in precious metals was largely confined to major centres such as Makkah, Jeddah and the Gulf ports. Metalwork was often imported from Oman and Yemen. Distinctive designs evolved in central Arabia and regional styles emerged in, for example, Qasim and Sudayr. Until the second quarter of the twentieth century, it was customary for every male to regard himself as properly dressed only when armed – with dagger or rifle or both – for ceremonial rather than defensive purposes.

While rifles were imported from Europe, local craftsmen set to work to customise them substantially, enhancing with inlay of silver or precious stones, inscribing, and frequently adding a large bulbous shoulder rest to the end of the butt.

Below:

Brass, wood and leather are the traditional materials for decorated shields. The leather is of camel hide, and the wood is often tamarisk.

Above and left:

Powder horns take their design with surprising literalness from the shape of ram's horns. The silversmith's craft in Arabia has for centuries been lavished on the hilts of swords and daggers, and their sheaths.

Below:

With the introduction of firearms in the late eighteenth century, smiths and engravers turned their skills to the decoration of rifles.

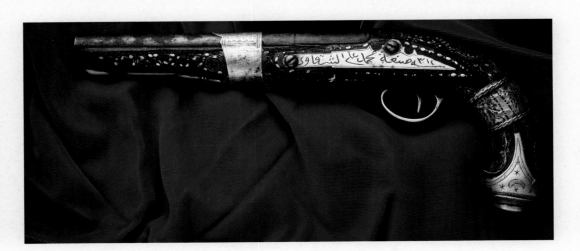

Embossing

The silversmith's arts of embossing and repoussé are put to use in these hilts and sheaths for the central Arabian daggers, in whose designs influences from Yemen, Oman and Turkey are evident.

panegyrics possessed an enormous moral force for the Bedouin, and had a regulatory effect within the community. The Prophet himself had to contend, through Muslim poets, with opponents who used the gift of poetry against him in Madinah. The first revelations to Mohammad were spoken in rhymed prose consisting of short phrases. These were taken down during his lifetime and were grouped into chapters which became collectively known as the Recitation, or Qur'an. There is no trace of Arabic prose before Islam, and although examples in the same form may have existed before, they were never written down. It was only the special nature of Mohammad's messages which caused them to be recorded.

The Holy Book's concern was not to produce a literary work, but to communicate the meaning which formed itself in it. To do this, the Qur'an initially employed a forceful, rhythmic and rhyming prose, for example: *"We have taught Muhammad no poetry, nor does it beseem him to be a poet. This is but a warning, an eloquent Qur'an to admonish the living and to pass judgement on the unbelievers."* Qur'an XXXVI, 69. Islam gathered in not only the poetic traditions but the practice of pilgrimage. Makkah's sanctity, reaffirmed and redefined by Muhammad, had attracted pilgrims from very ancient times. The last stopping place on the route from the south, lying somewhere between Ta'if and Makkah, was the fabled town of Ukhaz. Here, during the four-month season of the "holy truce", travellers gathered to meet their fellows, to trade, to recuperate for the last leg of their journey, and to recite. Poems were composed in honour of the powerful and were paid for in gold and silver. Swift fame was guaranteed to the successful poet. Here first developed the *Qasidah*, the ode in celebration of desert heroes – "appearing with Homeric suddenness", as Philip Hitti, the historian, has written, "and surpassing the *Iliad* and *Odyssey* in metrical complexity and elaboration."

Unquestionably, the poetic rhythms have been influenced by the gait of the camel. First to emerge was the rhythmic prose of the sages and travelling poets. From such prose grew the *Rajaz*, the four or six beat metre, rhymed prose for the father and song for the mother, spoken or sung to

were cultivated. The nomad jealously nurtured his language as his single unalienable good. By nature he was, and is, a rhetorician. The poet, the man of eloquence, was prized almost above all others in the community. His gifts and powers, believed to have been inspired by spirits, had already evolved a complex art form.

Poets sang of their lives, loves and land, but they also served as promulgators of the virtues and merits of their own tribes. The obligations of social values such as hospitality, generosity and courage were a matter of honour. Failure to uphold this unwritten code resulted in insult, and it was in this respect that poetic

The ardah *is the traditional sword dance of the Arabian peninsula (shown **above, left**). Accompanied by a chant and rhythmic drumming, it is generally a celebration of victory.*

the lilt of travel by camelback. And so eloquence was, and has been ever since, allowed its place in Arabian culture. The flow of poetry and well turned precepts has continued down the centuries, sagas of battles, journeys, loves and loyalties, moral tales and aphorisms as guides to the conduct of life, passed by word of mouth, from generation to generation, sometimes sung or chanted, sometimes accompanied by the stringed *rababa*. The *rababa*, just one of a variety of musical instruments which still play their part in modern Saudi life, has a quadrilateral sound-box covered with skin and is played with a horsehair bow to accompany heroic or love songs. It is the traditional instrument of the nomadic Bedouin. The *oud* (from which the English word "lute" derives) is still being made and sold in Arabian *suqs* and played at gatherings by young men. Its wooden sound-box is intricately decorated and beautiful. The *oud* was popular in the golden age of Arabic music, the Abbasid court of the years AD 750-850, and at that time known as the *amir at-tarab*, or the prince of enchantment. Drums are played at women's gatherings after weddings, accompanied by increasingly frenzied dancing. This tradition probably has an African origin. Men's sword-dancing, however, is not accompanied by music, only by hand-clapping and chanting.

In Saudi Arabia today dance is a common expression of communal rejoicing within men-only or women-only groups. Men celebrate during festivals such as the Eid by dancing in lines, advancing and retreating, flourishing their traditional swords in the air. Women celebrate spontaneously at any time of day but most commonly at the parties they hold at wedding gatherings. The dance is the stately forward and backward-stepping measure accompanied by the waving of scarves held in one hand. This is often an opportunity for a young girl to display her grace and beauty to potential mothers-in-law.

Craftsmanship

The nomadic life of the desert has always existed in interdependence with the settled life of the oasis or well watered south-west or the cities and ports. No Saudi Arabian settlement was without its hereditary lines of craftsmen: silversmiths, bronze-smiths, brass-smiths, gunsmiths and swordsmiths, potters and weavers and dyers, makers of incense burners and coffee mortars, makers and players of musical instruments. In the earlier past would have been found fletchers and bow-makers, and specialists in the manufacture of intricate

Coffee – its preparation almost as much as its consumption – has become over the ages a ritual among Arabs. Traditionally, each time a guest came, the beans were roasted, cooled on a wooden tray (mubarrad), *ground in a mortar* (yadd al-hamam), *tipped into boiling water and poured into a heated coffee pot* (dallah); *cardamom was added.*

Coffee is served in small cups without handles. It is the tradition for a guest to accept three cups (each containing about four sips), before 'wobbling' the cup as a signal that no more is desired.

Home Utensils

This coffee pot (dallah), *made in Hofuf more than 50 years ago, is of typical shape found across the peninsula.*

Incense is burned in a mahkhara *(as above, of wood, decorated with brass tacks and mirrors) and passed around to signal the end of a feast.*

Pots and pitchers, thrown on traditional potter's wheels and glazed, follow similar styles across Arabia.

This copper incense burner was made in Makkah, and is a fine example of traditional Islamic craftmanship.

These pestles and mortars, used for grinding spices and khol *are said to have originated in the Western Province.*

This basket for carrying water is made of tightly coiled fibres and caulked inside with clay. The outer case is of wood and leather.

Highly decorated brass-bound chests are a distinctive product of the Gulf area. Such chests were in the past part of the dowry of a newly-wed bride.

*Weaving has not always been the preserve of the settled communities (as shown **left**) but was also, until the 1960s, performed on mobile looms by the Bedouin tribeswomen, creating cloth for tent walls (as **left**), clothing, or saddlebags (**below, left**).*

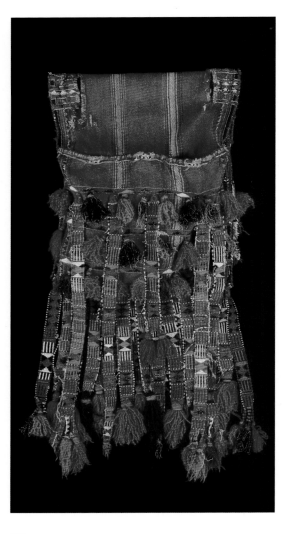

bird traps. And in the ancient past – revealed today in the Riyadh Museum of Archaeology and Ethnography – elegant stone tools were worked by the Neolithic inhabitants of the Rub al-Khali and Eastern Province.

The main centres, above all Makkah, would attract those with the finer skills: calligraphers and illuminators of holy manuscripts, ceramicists and workers in gold and silver thread, fine leatherworkers, cabinet-makers and chest-makers (this was a speciality of the Gulf, with its seafaring tradition), and those skilled in embossing and engraving, especially of guns. Many of these crafts were carried on in the tribes. Today they have largely been supplanted by imported, mass-produced goods. But the day of the Saudi craftsman is not done, for discerning collectors prize quality "Arabian" handiwork. Metal-working remains a skill honoured by townsfolk, villagers and Bedouin alike.

Bedouin jewellery

For centuries jewellery has formed an integral part of female attire in Arabia. The jewellery is both a woman's personal capital and dowry, and plays a part at the celebration of matrimony and at the approach of motherhood. A portion of a woman's bridal settlement is paid in jewellery; thereafter this becomes part of her personal wealth to keep or dispose of as she will. It is also customary for a woman to be presented with new pieces of jewellery whenever she bears a son. A Bedouin bride's dowry will still largely comprise a rich mass of silver jewellery. At her wedding she may be heavily caparisoned with headpieces and collars, earrings and necklaces, bangles and bracelets, besides amulets and belts. Since red, blue and green are regarded as protective, the silverware is often inset with amber, coral, lapis lazuli, garnets, agate, carnelian or turquoise. The individual pieces are wrought anew for each bride, and as a rule all are melted down at her death. Yet the designs (so widely admired today throughout the world) have remained extraordinarily constant for hundreds, indeed thousands, of years, as pre-Islamic grave relics demonstrate. Necklaces, frequently adorned with such ancient motifs

*A camel-borne litter is made up of a frame of wood bound with leather (**bottom, right**) over which a cloth is draped and fixed (**bottom left**). The larger such sheltered enclosure for the cherished womenfolk (**right**) is known as the* maksar *(or* howdaj*).*

as hand charms and crescents, have long stood as a symbol for love in romantic poetry. Many other jewellery forms are decorated with relief work which may include granulation, filigree, repoussé or niello details. Chain links and complex wire work based on the figure "8" are also common, as are bells and coinage of all sorts. Pictorial symbols and their stylized geometric equivalents, such as hands, crescents and triangles, are frequently found in Saudi jewellery and, as in much other Islamic art, provide protection from evil (the crescent's power in this respect is mentioned in Isaiah 3:8). The sign of the hand (the so-called hand of Fatima, daughter of the Prophet Mohammad) is closely associated with the number five representing the five tenets of Islam; a combination of related pieces worn together often offers an allusion to this.

The Maria Teresa thaler, the coinage of the Austro-Hungarian Empire, served until recently as the currency of Yemen, Oman and parts of Saudi Arabia. It has traditionally been incorporated into jewellery, prized for its symbolic as well as its monetary value.

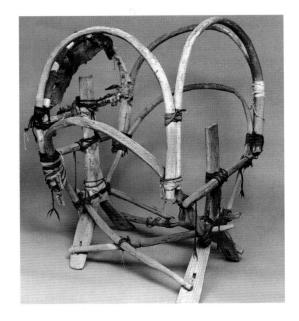

Jewellery

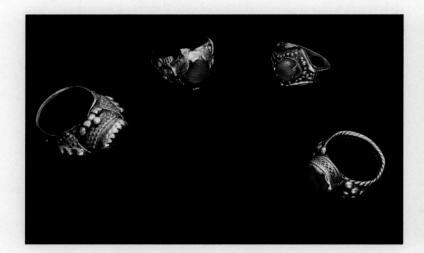

Traditional Bedouin jewellery had a role in tribal life far beyond mere adornment. It was a measure of the family's wealth, and to this day forms part of a bride's dowry, a badge of her married status. It is augmented by fresh pieces when the wife bears a son.

These pieces demonstrate a range of the craftsmanship of jewellers across Arabia. Silver is annealed and worked with techniques of chasing and repoussé into rings, bracelets and anklets (**above, right**) or adorned with filigree (**below**). Turquoise, coral and coloured glass are set into the metal, which in the case of the necklace (**left**) is gold plated.

The belt (**opposite**) is a woven silver band onto which are laid flat sections, decorated with rosettes, inlaid glass beads and applied filigree work; cast bells hang on chains.

Arts and Culture: Present and Future

The traditional arts and culture of Saudi Arabia are kept alive by the annual Heritage and Cultural Festival held outside Riyadh at Janadriyah every winter, under the auspices of the National Guard and the patronage of the King. The festival begins with a traditional camel race and continues with performances of traditional music and dance and exhibitions of traditional crafts such as weaving and pottery.

The organisations responsible for overseeing the arts in the Kingdom are the Saudi Arabian Society for Culture and the Arts, the General Presidency for Youth Welfare and the King Fahd Cultural Centre. These are now all under the auspices of the newly-created Ministry of Culture and Information, formed in May 2003. The roles of the individual organisations overlap to some extent at present: in future they will be unified under one authority, the Ministry.

The General Presidency has a particular responsibility for nurturing the interests of the young, encouraging every aspect of their development. To this end it has sponsored a range of cultural activities including exhibitions of art and calligraphy at home and abroad (in Kuwait, Europe, Asia and India) and poetry and essay competitions, and has established clubs to encourage art, literature, drama and folklore all over the country. These literary clubs have been experiencing marked success in promoting events such as literary evenings, symposia, lectures, book publishing, exhibitions and folkloric festivals (of which Janadriyah, referred to above, is the most prominent).

The King Abdul Aziz Research Centre in Riyadh contains the Kingdom's historical archives and is a fundamental reference source. It makes available books, periodicals and audio-visual material and is attempting to revive Islamic and Arab heritage. Its holdings now include 78,000 books and 18,000 manuscripts. It also undertakes

resource projects such as preparing a "Who's Who" for the century and holds documentary films and audio-visual tapes. There is another huge national library, the King Fahd Library, which assembles documents of a scientific nature and is compiling a catalogue of Saudi authors, both male and female.

The completion of the King Abdul Aziz Historical Centre in Riyadh in 1999 in time for the celebration of the Kingdom's foundation, represents a marvellous architectural achievement. It preserves the traditional architecture of old Riyadh, especially the Murabba Palace which forms its core, within a modern setting which now contains the national archaeological collection.

The further aim of the Government in respect to Saudi culture is to unify cultural services within one institution, as mentioned above, and to continue to preserve and sustain traditional – and often endangered – culture, arts and architecture.

Opposite:
The pottery makers in Jebel Gharra, outside Hofuf, keep alive a tradition that can be traced back to ancient times.

Right:
The superb craftsmanship of the Makkan veil in gold and pearls dates from the last century.

4

The People, Their Habitat and Way of Life

Saudi Arabians today are largely city dwellers. They lead a very different life from that of their forbears, who for the most part lived either in settled agricultural communities, or as nomads moving widely with their flocks and camels in search of pasture. Yet in rural areas, something of the ancient style and pattern of life prevails.

With Saudi Arabia's population growth at one of the highest rates in the world and with the unstoppable allure of modernisation, the way of life will continue to evolve, bringing further dramatic changes ... and challenges.

While the peninsula is widely known for its harsh desert reaches, there are large areas of greenery, either around the oases to the east, or, more so as the terrain rises to meet the mountains of the south-west. The settled agricultural lifestyle of the communities that thrive on such areas of fertility continues to this day. Here, a young girl guides her livestock on the Tihama.

Left:
The inhabitants of Arabia today are generally descended either from the fiercely independent Bedouin tribes which for centuries scoured the deserts for their meagre bounty, or from the cosmopolitan settled communities which thrived on the trade routes up and down the east and west coasts, or occupied Makkah.

Traditional Arabian Societies

Both archaeology and the ancient pre-Islamic records of Arabia provide evidence of a tribally organised, camel-herding society which already by 1000 BC spanned the spectrum of nomadic and settled lifestyles. During the centuries of the high civilisation of the ancient south-west, nomad and settler were already interacting in much the same way as they have done until recent times. The familiar patterns of conflict and interdependence, in which each relied upon the other for essential goods and services but could at the same time come into conflict over water and grazing rights, have thus marked their relations for some 3,000 years and probably more. It is this interdependence which gives the lie to the notion that nomadism, because it is in some sense more 'primitive', must predate the emergence of settled life. In fact, the archaeology of the region suggests that both lifestyles evolved in parallel as ways of exploiting scarce resources to the full. It is clear that there are not, and never have been, nomads in Arabia who had complete economic independence. They have always relied on the settled areas for a proportion of their food. There has always been interchange between the desert and the town, with settlers adopting a nomadic or semi-nomadic lifestyle and nomads taking over settlements and becoming farmers and traders, in response to prevailing environmental, social and political conditions. Hence settlements in what is today Saudi Arabia have always reflected their tribal origins: towns were often organised in quarters corresponding to the tribal origins of their inhabitants. The same tribe could frequently include both settled and nomadic components. But the conditions of settled life tended to produce a more sophisticated culture than that of the nomadic tribes. In one sense the rise of Islam can be seen as a clash between the aspirations of the town and the customs of the tribal nomads, whose religion had been polytheistic and animist. The early Muslims were essentially townsmen who sought to replace the limited loyalties of

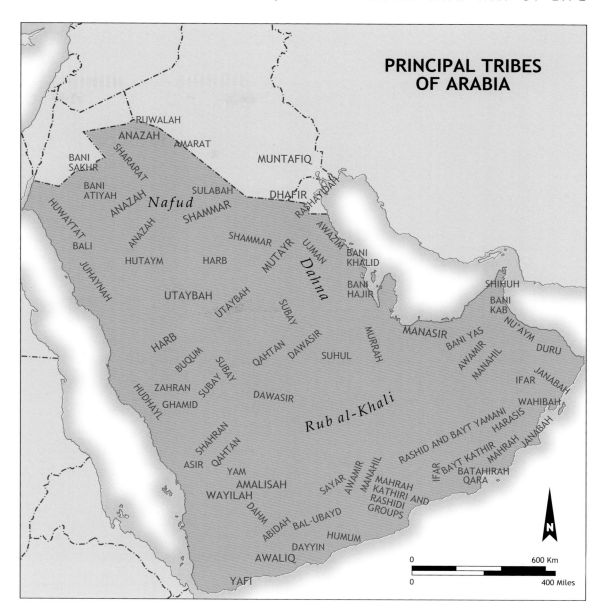

PRINCIPAL TRIBES OF ARABIA

the tribe with a greater one to the Islamic state under God, and with the idea of the brotherhood of all Muslims.

With the Dawn of Islam, the old tribal virtues were replaced by a divinely inspired ethical code. Many of the customs of early tribal life were banned, such as the killing of unwanted female children, and the veneration of certain rocks and trees. The exacting of revenge was discouraged, to be supplanted by the administration of law. Oral poetry lost its special character and, in any case, was soon outshone by the glories of Arabic literature. However, tribalism itself persisted down the centuries in Arabia in a counterpoint to the efforts of enlightened settled rulers and jurists to broaden its scope. By the twentieth century, some of the values of nomadic life had changed very little, with Bedouin often placing their

Above:

The structure of the tribe in social life is evident from the earliest records of life on the peninsula. Naturally the role of tribe in society has evolved over the course of time and with the various religious and foreign influences coming to bear. But tribal allegiance is still very evident and underpins social relationships in even an urban setting.

Bedouin

The Bedouin (*bedu* in Arabic) long lived in one of the harshest and inhospitable environments in the world: extreme heat by day, sharp cold by night, scant supplies of water and scarce food resources. The resulting social structures were very strong: small groups living in close harmony, fiercely independent, resistant to outside influence, yet paradoxically extremely generous to the passing visitor. The strength of character that developed from living in such conditions, as well as the reputation for hospitality, are still greatly valued and the traditions are consciously carried on in modern Saudi society.

For the most part, the Bedouin themselves no longer lead the same lives as before, and have accepted the value of hospitals, schooling and the trappings of life in more settled urban communities where food is no longer in short supply and air conditioning mitigates the desert heat. Four-wheel drive vehicles have largely supplanted the camel as the preferred mode of transport. Yet the camel still has a part to play, including as a source of milk and meat.

tribal obligations over their duty to Islam. The economic changes of recent times have, more than any other factor, wrought a change in the tribal scene. The motor car spelt the end of Bedouin wealth based on camel and horse breeding, and the rise of the oil industry has attracted them into new occupations, giving them skills and education in the process. But the subordination of tribal values to those of Islam, and the triumph of settled values over nomadic ones which were its inevitable accompaniment, traces its real origin in Saudi Arabia to the rise of the Wahhabi reform movement in the eighteenth century and the establishment of the First Saudi State under the leadership of the House of Saud. King Abdul Aziz's achievement in the early part of the last century in unifying much of Arabia was but the latest, if the most far-reaching, manifestation of this process.

Regions

Saudi Arabia is divided for administrative purposes into five regions: the Central Region (Najd), the Western Region (Hejaz); the Southern Region, (Tihama and Asir); the Eastern Region (al-Hasa and Qatif); and the Rub al-Khali, or Empty Quarter. To this we have added, for the purposes of this book, the Northern Region. Each has its own very distinct character. There are also 13 administrative areas: al-Baha, al-Jawf, Asir, Eastern, Ha'il, Jizan, Madinah, Makkah, Najran, Northern Border, Qasim, Riyadh and Tabouk.

Central Region

The People

For centuries the nomadic people of the central desert regions lived in a symbiotic relationship with the settled people of the towns and farming settlements, whereby the nomadic Bedouin exchanged their produce of goat and sheep, leather and woven articles for agricultural produce, fruit and vegetables grown in the wadi farms and settlements, and in times of trouble and internecine strife the

nomadic people would even seek refuge within the towns. Now that prosperity has come, with the advent of oil wealth, to all the people of the Kingdom, the old way of life of nomadic people moving north in the summer for the lusher pastures of northern Saudi Arabia or southern Iraq and Syria, and south again when the rains made the desert of central Arabia fertile, has largely disappeared. Modern life has brought comfort and wealth for all, but many feel something has been lost with the passing of the virtues engendered by the harsh conditions of desert life. Such a way of life still existed in the early part of the twentieth century, as writers such as Wilfred Thesiger who travelled with the Bedouin in the 1940s have described, (*see* The Rub al-Khali, page 151). The advent of the motor vehicle in the 1930s, contemporaneously with the start of Saudi Arabia's own petroleum industry, spelt the end of the horse and camel as the principal means of human transportation, and with it the transformation of professional opportunities.

The old tribal allegiances, as we have noted, remain a strong force in modern Saudi society, in towns as well as desert communities. In the past, towns were often organised into quarters corresponding to the tribal origins of their inhabitants and frequently the same tribe would include both settled and nomadic components.

The History

The Central Region, the province of Najd, is at the heart of Saudi Arabia and its history has been central to that of the history of the Kingdom. Its inhabitants, Najdis, have the reputation of being austere and strict adherents of Islam. Character is frequently shaped by climate and geography and Najd has a harsh climate of extreme summer heat by day, often dropping dramatically at night – and very cold winter nights. Geographically isolated by the mountain barrier of the Hejaz to the west and sand on the other three sides, Najd means "highland". Its only recorded invasion was that by Ibrahim in 1818.

Members of tribes calling themselves sons of Qahtan or southern Arabs moved northwards and intermingled with the sons of

Adnan or northern Arabs whom they found there. The Najdis of today are in the main the offspring of these northern and southern stocks. In other parts of the Arab world, Arabs have assimilated with the indigenous peoples, but in Najd they have maintained a thorough Arabness which is perhaps their most distinguishing characteristic. As the new religion of Islam advanced in the Arabian peninsula, it met resistance in central Najd where, soon after the death of the Prophet Muhammad, a false prophet, Musaylimah the Liar, preached a heretical creed. To overcome him, Abu Bakr, the first Caliph, had to call upon his finest general, Khalid ibn al-Walid, the Sword of God. Once the Najdis came to understand the spiritual message and values of Islam, however, they devoted themselves enthusiastically to its cause. The bane of the region, however, remained for centuries civil strife and almost incessant feuding, town against town, tribe against tribe, nomadic bands against settled communities. This feuding militated against the formation of a powerful and durable state, and the absence of such a state meant that there was no authority to enforce effectively the Sacred Law of Islam and hold the people of Najd to orthodoxy.

As time went by, backsliding became common. Many Najdis embraced new beliefs abhorrent to the true spirit of Islam. In the eighteenth century a religious scholar of central Najd, Sheikh Muhammad bin Abd al-Wahhab, determined to bring Najd and the rest of Arabia back to the original and undefiled form of Islam. To achieve this purpose he allied himself with Muhammad ibn Saud, the ruler of Dir'iyyah, as this work records on pages 55-6. (This alliance survived in the person of the late King Faisal, who was descended on the paternal side from the ruler and on the maternal side from the Sheikh.) This alliance between the House of Saud and the reforming Sheikh gave impetus to the First Saudi State which, from its capital base Dir'iyyah, conquered much of the Arabian peninsula. The ruins of this first Saudi capital, Dir'iyyah, in the Wadi Hanifah, retains vestiges of huge mud-brick buildings in which large numbers of visitors and representatives of client states bearing tribute were received. For a period of about 40 years Dir'iyyah was wealthy and

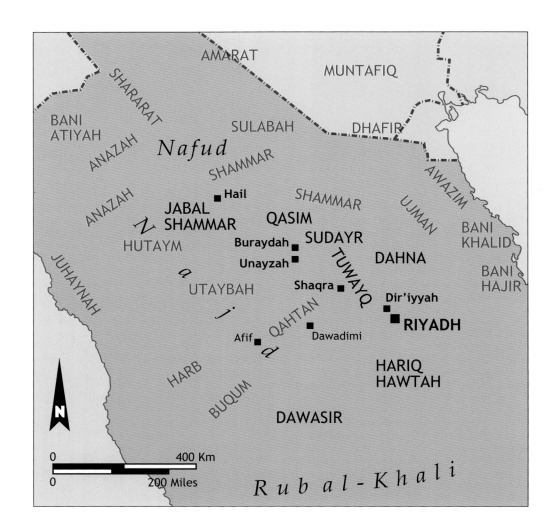

powerful. However, this success, in particular the conquest of Makkah and Madinah by the Wahhabis, attracted the enmity of the Ottoman Empire and a force under Ibrahim Pasha invaded Najd in 1818 and destroyed the power of the al-Saud, reducing Dir'iyyah to the picturesque ruined state seen today. The al-Saud moved their base to nearby Riyadh but in 1871 Muhammad bin Rashid of Ha'il seized much of Najd and al-Hasa, and in 1891 forced the then head of the family of al-Saud, Abdul Rahman bin Faisal, to flee. With his son, the future King Abdul Aziz ibn Saud, Abdul Rahman eventually sought refuge in Kuwait.

It was from there that the young Abdul Aziz ibn Saud launched his daring raid in 1902 to retake Riyadh. Ibn Saud made Riyadh the capital of the Saudi state and from this base sallied forth to subdue the different parts of the peninsula which now constitute the Kingdom, founded in 1932. It is almost certain that, without the unifying force of Ibn Saud, the far flung communities that today form Saudi Arabia would have evolved separately.

The Towns

Riyadh

Riyadh's original reason for settlement was its potential for cultivation, hence its name al-Riyadh, 'the gardens'. Situated in the centre of Najd, on a sedimentary plateau 600 metres above sea level, at the confluence of Wadi Hanifah and its tributaries Wadi Aysan and Wadi Batha, it has a very dry climate and low rainfall, but a good underground water supply made it one of the few naturally fertile areas in the Kingdom outside the southwest. There has been a settlement in the Wadi Hanifah on the site of modern Riyadh, since the fifth century AD. This was known as Hajar until about the twelfth century when the name Riyadh was first used. At that time Riyadh was a stopping point on the east-west pilgrim route to Makkah.

Some time after the foundation of the town of Dir'iyyah in the Wadi Hanifah in the fifteenth century, Riyadh gave way to Dir'iyyah as the chief town of the area. The

*That an independent town with lively streets and a vibrant community could grow up in the heart of the Najd desert was always an intriguing testament to the power water has to bring life. Before ever the oil boom brought untold wealth to this remote inland capital, however, the city had flourished from the east-west pilgrim and trade routes, an essential stopping point on a difficult journey. With the advent of oil the city soon burst the age old frontiers of what is now known as the "old town" (seen **left** and **below** in pictures from the 1950s). Riyadh expanded to become the metropolis of just under 5 million citizens that it is today.*

Opposite:
Tribal distribution in central Saudi Arabia.

Dir'iyyah

The ruins of the first Saudi capital, Dir'iyyah, in the Wadi Hanifah near Riyadh, retain samples of huge mud-brick buildings in which large numbers of visitors and representatives of client states bearing tribute were received at the end of the eighteenth century. For a period of about 40 years Dir'iyyah was wealthy and powerful. However this success, in particular the conquest of Makkah and Madinah by the Wahhabis, attracted the enmity of the Ottoman empire and a force under Ibrahim Pasha invaded Najd in 1818 and destroyed the power of the al-Saud, reducing Dir'iyyah to the picturesque ruined state seen today, parts of which have been loyally restored and preserved.

The architectural achievement was significant. The remarkably high, long walls, the tall towers, the pillars and ornamentation, were all on a grandiose scale that had not previously been achieved in central Arabia. Nor were they, as long as mud and brick remained the primary construction materials, to be repeated on the same ambitious scale following the destruction of Dir'iyyah. The illustrations here give a flavour of the distinctive style which was developed by the masterbuilders who constructed the city, notably the inset triangular decorative motifs and the ribbed crenellations. Stone, usually only part of the foundations of a Najdi dwelling, was used more extensively in Dir'iyyah, with regular limestone courses masked by mud rendering. The real architectural achievement of Dir'iyyah, however, was the palace itself, of which only the foundations were of stone, with mud for everything above. Many of these walls, rising to a considerable height, still stand today, testament to the exacting standards of the craftsmen who built them.

Below:

The interior of the Subalat Mudi mosque.

Below:

A section of the Bayt al-Mal treasury wall.

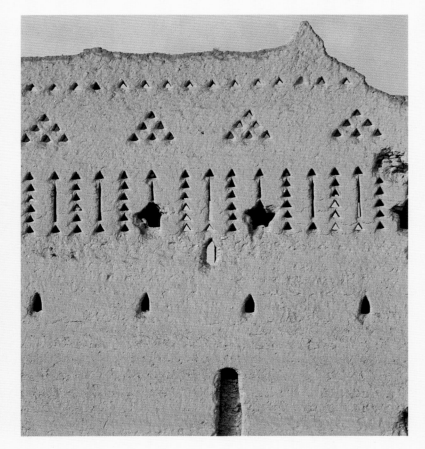

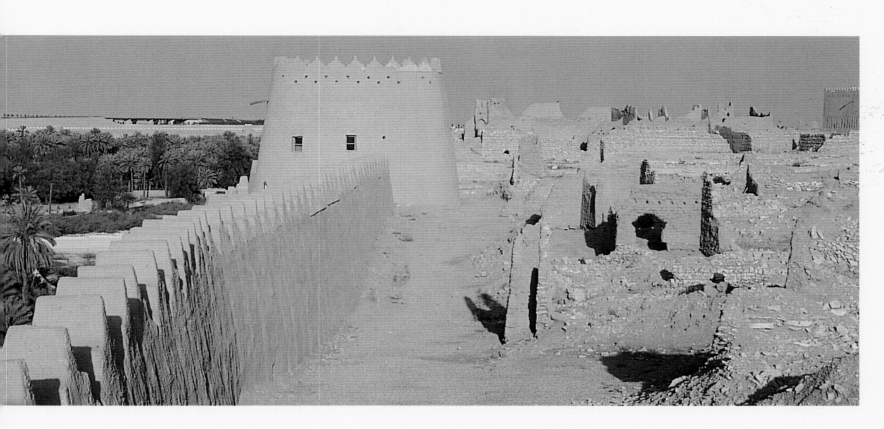

Above: *An interior view of Dir'iyyah's defensive outer wall.*
Below: *A typical Najdi door in Turayf.*

Below:
The magnificent Palace of Sa'd, built on three storeys.

rise of the first Saudi state, based on Dir'iyyah, has been described above. The al-Saud captured Riyadh in 1773 but lost it after the Ottoman Turks destroyed Dir'iyyah and took control of Najd in 1818. The control of Riyadh passed in and out of the hands of the al-Saud during the nineteenth century but was finally lost to the Rashid of Ha'il in 1891, when the al-Saud were forced to flee. In January 1902 the young Abdul Aziz ibn Saud seized the Musmak fortress and hence the city, which became the base from which he conquered the vast area from the Arabian Gulf to the Red Sea which in 1932 became the Kingdom of Saudi Arabia.

At the time Abdul Aziz took Riyadh, the town was surrounded by a thick mud wall about 7 metres high, punctuated at intervals by bastions and gates. Inside it was a maze of twisting alleys, some so narrow that it was difficult for two men to walk abreast. In the centre was the market with, on one side, a large

mosque and, on the other, the great fortress-palace which served as the seat of government. All the buildings were made of the same mud-brick as the walls.

At first change came so rapidly after the discovery of oil that the old and the new were jumbled together: in the 1970s the cars and trucks of Batha Street moved in a cacophany of horns, stirring up dust from the broken pavements. Now, however, broad highways carry traffic rapidly around and across the huge and still expanding city, new housing pushing the limits ever further into the desert.

The city today covers some 1,600 square kilometres and has a population of 4.7 million. As the centre of government and a major international commercial city, Riyadh is well served with excellent hotels, roads, shops, communications and fine new buildings. Many of these blend traditional Arabian styles with the most modern styles of architecture. Notable examples of this are the King Khalid

In the heart of the Najd lies the capital, Riyadh, (literally 'the gardens') so named because of the greenery it derived from underground aquifers. Over the course of the city's development, from mud-brick structures such as the Musmak fortress to the towers of glass and steel which now overshadow it, maintenance and expansion of the green areas has been a point of pride, as seen here in a quiet corner of the Diplomatic Quarter (above).

Museums

The nation's heritage and history are loyally preserved in the National Museum, part of an impressive modern complex near the old town of Riyadh, and the country's flagship museum. From the meticulously landscaped gardens, to the dramatic architecture of the building itself, no expense has been spared in ensuring a pleasurable learning experience.

Parties of school children are a regular feature, and the trip provides the young with a rare insight into how the modern nation came into being. The exhibits start with the prehistory of the peninsula - the skeleton of a mastodon *(bottom right)* would have roamed the once fertile plains, since burnt to desert sands. Also included are artefacts of early civilisations, such as the hollow bronze lion's head *(below right)* found in Najran that would have been the product of sophisticated casting some 2,500 years ago, the marble bowl *(top right)* dating from 2,000 years ago, also from Najran, and the woman's head *(below left)* from Al-Is in the Hejaz. The coverage runs through the coming of Islam and right up to the recent past, showing the household crafts *(centre right)* and fishing vessels *(bottom left)* that would have been part of day-to-day life in coastal villages less than 100 years ago.

International Airport (now serving over 8.3 million passengers a year), the Foreign Ministry Complex, the huge tent-like structure of the King Fahd International Stadium and the Diplomatic Quarter. In place of the former gardens there are now a number of parks open to the public: a particularly successful example of this is the rock-cut path which runs around the edge of the Diplomatic Quarter, interspersed with little gardens and playgrounds. In the centre of the old city, where the Musmak fortress still stands (now a museum to the life of King Abdul Aziz), Dira square connects the new Grand Mosque to the *Hukm* or Governorate. Around the old Murabba Palace lies the King Abdul Aziz Historical Centre development, opened to celebrate the Kingdom's centenary, incorporating an outstandingly well-designed museum, library and restored palace and other mud buildings.

The other major towns of the central region are Buraidah and Unayzah.

Buraidah

Buraidah is the regional capital of Qasim and an area now producing quantities of wheat in circular fields, irrigated by underground water. It is also known for its camel market – the largest in the world – as well as for the largest pharmaceutical factory in the Middle East.

Unayzah

Unayzah, the twin city of Buraidah, is another town which has become rich in agricultural produce such as wheat, barley and fruit, thanks to the Government policy of irrigation from geological water sources.

*The architecture of Riyadh, although incorporating many modern elements, had no skyscrapers until the almost simultaneous erection of the two office towers on Olaya Street. The first to be completed, in 2001, was that of the Al-Faisaliyya complex (**above**), which also incorporates a five-star hotel and shopping mall, seen on the left of the picture, all built to the design of the British architect Norman Foster. The second, the Kingdom Tower (**right**), known for the 'bottle opener' top wide enough to allow the passage of a Cessna light aircraft through the gap, was opened to the public the following year. Sponsored by Prince al-Walid bin Talal bin Abdul Aziz, it soars to a height of 302 metres, 28 metres higher than Al-Faisaliyya at 274 metres.*

*The spectacular growth of Riyadh since the 1960s has demanded highly sophisticated city planning and a complex road programme to handle the immense demands of peak times (**below left**). The municipality has sought to increase the appeal of pedestrian movement, like that of the corniche-style walkways on Abdul Aziz Street (**left, above**). Riyadh is now a city of several elegant precincts, like that of north Olaya, served by the green expanses of Salaam Park (**right** and **below, right**).*

The Architectural Heritage of Najd

In Najd the main building material is unfired mud-brick; the completed wall is made smooth by the application of mud-plaster. These walls are very thick, and provide insulation against the extremities of the local climate. The roofing consists of wooden beams, usually of tamarisk, with palm matting or twigs spread above. This is covered with a layer of mud. Stone is used only as the foundation of a house or in fortifications.

The Najdi mosque consists of a walled enclosure around an open courtyard, with a covered sanctuary built against the *qibla* wall. Cut into this wall is the *mihrab* niche, which projects beyond the back wall of the mosque, an arrangement common in both ancient and modern mosques in Saudi Arabia. The roof of the sanctuary rests on colonnades with keel arches, the number of colonnades depending on the mosque's size and importance. Some mosques have underground prayer-chambers for use in winter. In the Riyadh area and southern Najd, one or two staircases nearly always give access to the roof; in this area the mosques are either without minarets, or have only a diminutive tower over the staircase to the roof. In Sudayr and Qasim, however, minarets are tall and cylindrical.

Najdi houses are often built around a central courtyard, with only a few openings on to the street, thus maintaining the privacy of family life. The buildings have one, two or three storeys depending on their importance. The entrances to the houses are closed by large rectangular wooden doors, and the windows by wooden shutters. Both shutters and doors are decorated with incised geometric patterns picked out in colour, or by geometrics burned into the pale wooden surface. The only other external decorations are rows of V-shaped mouldings on the walls, and crenellations which vary in design from area to area. Elaborately-shaped mud finials grace the corners of the houses. The position of the reception rooms varies. In most larger houses the lower rooms are used for storage, and visitors are received upstairs. However, rooms designed to receive guests appear in Sadus and Unayzah on both the ground floor and upper storey. In a corner of these receptions rooms there is usually a small hearth for coffee-making, with shelves above.

A key feature of the use of mud, as opposed to the brick, steel and concrete used in the modern construction work, is the need for ongoing care and attention, patching up crumbling walls, repairing storm damage. This chore, itself the rationale behind the materials used in most contemporary buildings, paradoxically ensures the longevity of the building, enabling a family home to be maintained and developed from generation to generation indefinitely.

*Sustained care is taken to ensure that modern architectural structures are obeisant to the motifs and themes which are the region's heritage. The foreground tower of the Dukhna Gate (**right**), one of two at the southern end of Riyadh city, is the inspiration for the modern structure behind, and care is taken to ensure the two can live in harmony. The same distinctive crenellations adorn the courtyard walls of the Murabba Palace (**left and overleaf**).*

Murabba Palace Interior

The Murabba Palace was the late King Abdul Aziz's favourite residence, his home for 50 years. From its crenellated parapets in the heart of the old city, he witnessed Riyadh's early growth. Here he gave audiences every week to any of his subjects with a grievance to bring to him. The grounds outside the Palace served as a gathering place on market and feast days. The Palace itself welcomed State visitors. It featured in most early photographs of the town. In recent years it has been scrupulously renovated inside and out, giving today's visitor an insight into day-to-day life in the heart of the Kingdom's royal government in the first half of the twentieth century. The Palace courtyard, reception room and exterior are pictured on this page and the previous two pages.

The discovery of oil brought both the wealth and the fuel for mechanised transport in the Kingdom. The camel, the perfect desert vehicle over thousands of years, was challenged almost overnight by the car (for basic transport) and tractors (for agricultural work). The result has been a huge increase in yield and the expansion of the agricultural industry over a far wider area. Traditions die hard, however, and camels still provide the driving force to pull water up from a rural well in Buraidah and to irrigate the fields.

Western Region

The People and their History

Traditionally, the people of western Arabia have linked the world of the Red Sea and Mediterranean with the interior. Of all the natural divisions into which the Kingdom may be split, the Western Province is the most diverse. It approximately corresponds to the region known as the Hejaz. It is a land of great variety where cultivated hilltops give way to seemingly endless desert, where steamy heat yields to bracing winds and frosts, and where townsmen live side-by-side with nomads. Over the whole area, the ebb and flow of many civilizations has left its impression on the people. Yet, out of all this diversity it is possible to identify a Hejazi, not by physical appearance or by way of life, but by a bond of historical and cultural associations. For centuries, the settlements have been linked by the passage of caravans bearing precious cargoes and

communities of the devout performing the *hajj*; by the years spent as an outlying province of the Ottoman Empire, and by 14 centuries of provisioning and serving the *Haramayn*, or Holy Cities. The origins and distribution of the Hejazi peoples have been strongly influenced by geography.

North of a line from Jeddah to Ta'if is a land of deserts: arid mineralized mountains or great sweeps of sand and stone. Where the fortunes of geology have yielded fresh water near the coast, and at a few points inland, settled communities of farmers, traders, fishermen or sailors have formed. But where aridity prevails then man has adapted to a way of life based on movement. In consequence, the northern Hejaz has never been able to support significant densities of population, with the one striking exception of Madinah, where water gushes out from beneath the great lava field of the Harrat al-Rahah. To the south of the Jeddah-Ta'if line is another world entirely. There, high above the stifling heat of the Tihama, the ascending winds of the

summer monsoon bring regular rains which have permitted the development of many hundreds of farming homesteads. Outward and downward from the mountains aridity prevails, and settlements become fewer until the wandering way of life prevails once more.

Although the word 'Hejaz' means barrier, the history of the area and its peoples belies the term. The barrier referred to is the Great Escarpment which runs along, rather than across, the Hejaz, dividing it from the interior plateaux. This same escarpment transforms the arid Hejaz into a natural corridor between the frankincense and myrrh country of Arabia Felix and the rich markets of the Fertile Crescent. Along this route a number of resting places and trading centres developed such as Makkah, Madinah, Khaybar and Tabuk, where water was available to sustain a settled population. Into these settlements came the merchant adventurers of the past: the Nabataeans in their rock-cut city of Medain Saleh; the Jews in their fortress towns of Yathrib and Khaybar. From later pre-Islamic times the city of Makkah held a special place as a centre of pilgrimage and culture: a role which was greatly emphasized after the *hajj* brought new racial and cultural strains into the Hejaz: as the word of the Prophet spread, so the diversity increased. Many who came stayed, while others brought their skills to the service of the pilgrimage: from India came the grain merchants to Jeddah; from Hadhramaut, the traders and importers; from Java the descendants of Muslim missionaries, and, from Turkey and Egypt, the soldiers to police the desert trails. Sometimes, as in Makkah and Jeddah, the ethnic types congregated into district *haras* or quarters of the city such as the Nusla Yamaniyya of Jeddah. Often, however, the individual groups were absorbed into the cosmopolitan embrace of the Hejazi way of life, only their names distinguishing their origins: the Tunsis (Tunisia), the Daghestanis, the Yamanis (Yemen) and the Misris (Egypt). Such are the demographic origins of cities like Jeddah, Makkah, Madinah, Ta'if and Yanbu.

In the smaller towns and oases of the north, a lasting symbiosis developed between the itinerant Bedouin such as the Bili, Huwaytat, Juhayna and the Harb and the settled farmers of

Opposite:

Jeddah, the principal port for visitors coming until recent times by sea on pilgrimage to the Holy Places, has also benefited from the north-south trade route – the former frankincense trails that follows the eastern seaboard of the Red Sea.

Above:

The capital of the Western region, however, lies inland. Madinah, the Prophet's birthplace, is seen above in a photograph taken in 1908.

Right:

Tribal distribution in western Saudi Arabia.

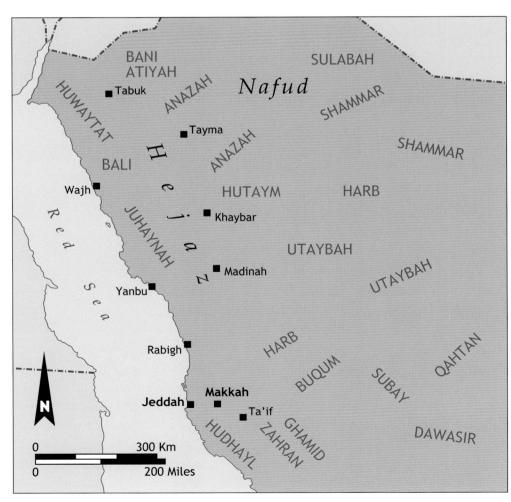

the agricultural oases. Very often the oases were dependencies of one or other Bedouin group and were peopled by slaves and their descendants brought from Somalia, Eritrea and the Swahili coast of East Africa. This introduced a negroid element into the ethnic diversity which already existed. In the south, along the coast, the African strain is strong and the Takarinah, or people of the Tihama plain, retain their distinctive thatched dwellings and racial features, though their African dialects have yielded to a universal use of Arabic. In the hamlets of the highlands, however, a Semitic homogeneity prevails, possibly because the farmers, pressed hard upon their small farms, could neither use nor support a slave population.

The Hejaz was traditionally the commercial heart of the country, deriving its wealth from pilgrims coming to Makkah and traders using the port of Jeddah. During the 1960s and 1970s, prosperity attracted increasing numbers of people into the Hejaz in several well-defined streams. At the same time, a clearly differentiated pattern of internal movement established and reinforced itself. From Syria, Palestine, Egypt, Lebanon, Iraq and Pakistan came the skilled and semi-skilled workers needed to fill the gaps created by sudden and rapid growth. They concentrated mostly in the cities and towns, but some, notably doctors and teachers, were sent into rural areas. This was seen by the Saudis as a stop-gap measure while the country trained its own qualified staff. For years, unskilled Yemenis flocked north to work on the building sites, while women from Ethiopia and Somalia came seeking domestic employment. Within the Hejaz the economic take-off had no less an impact on the indigenous population. The Bedouin largely quit their traditional pastoral wanderings and exchanged the camel caravan for the Mercedes truck, the goat-hair tent for a breeze-block house on the outskirts of a town or city. Here, too, job and origin remain allied: find a taxi driver and you have found a Bedouin.

Above:

While the Gulf, running along the eastern coast of Saudi Arabia, is a salty and shallow tract of water supporting relatively little wildlife, the Red Sea is home to a wide range of sea- and bird-life – flamingoes being a common sight near the coast north of Jeddah.

Opposite and overleaf:

The visit to the Grand Mosque in Madinah is traditionally the last action to be performed by pilgrims before they leave the country.

The Towns

Makkah al-Mukarrimah

Makkah al-Mukarrimah, 'the blessed', birthplace of the Prophet Muhammad, the place where God's message was first revealed to him and the city to which he returned after the migration to Madinah in 622 AD, is the holiest city of Islam. Towards Makkah Muslims all over the world, wherever they are, turn in prayer five times a day. Over three million Muslim pilgrims (*hajjis,*) make their way to Makkah each year. Many still enter the Kingdom through the port of Jeddah, 73 kilometres to the west; many more come in by air.

The most important building in Makkah is the Grand Mosque, in the courtyard of which stands the Ka'abah, the cube-shaped stone building which houses the Black Stone, a piece of meteorite sacred to Islam and the starting point for the seven circumambulations of the mosque which every *hajji* must complete.

In the monarch's role as Custodian of the Two Holy Places, King Fahd undertook a multimillion dollar programme of expansion and modernisation in Makkah to make the place of pilgrimage more accessible to ever greater numbers. The expanded Mosque can now hold over a million worshippers during Ramadan, *umrah* and *hajj*. The project added two new minarets.

Makkah's founding is attributed to the presence of the well opened in the desert by God to save the lives of Hagar and her son, Isma'il, from whom – with his father Abraham – the Arab race traces its descent. Before Islam it was already a place of pilgrimage as the Black Stone was held to have sacred significance.

Since Islam the pilgrimage has brought huge numbers of devout Muslims to the city, as it is one of the five pillars of Islam for a Muslim to make the pilgrimage to Makkah at least once in his lifetime. In the Middle Ages pilgrims often took months or even years to complete the arduous journey from the far corners of the Muslim world and many did not return home. The present inhabitants of Makkah are in part descended from these pilgrims and, as a result of this ethnic mix, the people of Makkah are considered amongst the most beautiful in Arabia. The city has vastly increased in size since the 1970s but all construction work must be done by Muslims as non-Muslims are not permitted to enter the Holy City.

Madinah al-Munawwarah

Madinah al-Munawwarah, the "shining city", lying 447 kilometres north of Makkah, is the second most holy city in Islam. It was to Madinah that the Prophet Muhammad and his followers, faced by the hostility of the Makkan merchants, departed in 622 (the year of the *Hijra* from which the Islamic calendar dates). The people of Madinah asked the Prophet to live amongst them and to arbitrate in their affairs, and this submission to the one God, Allah, marks the start of the Islamic era. The Prophet is buried in Madinah. The present city, like Makkah closed to non-Muslims, has the second holiest mosque in Islam. It too has been greatly expanded since the 1980s and now has the capacity to hold over a million worshippers. It remains a centre of religious learning, based on its Islamic University and famous library.

It is reported in the hadith *that the Prophet Mohammad personally took part in the original construction of the Prophet's Mosque (**left**) at Madinah. To this day, it contains the Prophet's tomb, as well as those of the first two Rightly Guided Caliphs, Abu Bakr and Omar.*

Through the ages, the structure has been regularly renovated and extended. Following major engineering work started in 1985 and lasting for almost a decade, the mosque area now has the capacity to hold up to one million worshippers at a time.

Left and opposite:
The Miqaat Mosque just outside Madinah is one of the main welcoming centres at which arriving pilgrims don the ihram *before travelling on to the Holy Cities.*

Jeddah

The "Bride of the Sea", founded by Caliph Uthman ibn Affan in 647, is today the largest port on the Red Sea, with a magnificent modern harbour. It is the most cosmopolitan of Saudi cities, owing to its status as the seaport and airport for *hajjis* visiting Makkah. Much of the traditional Arab architecture of Jeddah was pulled down to make way for modern office blocks, banks and apartments, but much also remains and has been restored, particularly in the old city.

Its position on the ancient incense and trade routes and its proximity to Makkah made Jeddah for centuries the wealthiest town in Arabia. Its commercial importance declined somewhat with the mounting sea power of Europe and in 1517 the town fell under the intermittent authority of the Ottoman Turks, as part of the domain of the Sharif of Makkah. However, the opening of the Suez Canal in 1869 proved a boon for Jeddah with its merchants handling a regular volume of commerce with other Arabian ports, India, Egypt, Africa and even Liverpool and

Marseilles. From this period date the many fine merchant family houses that survive in the old city. The most celebrated is Beit Nassif, home of the Nassif family for over a century until the house was passed to the care of the Government in the mid-1970s. Designed by a Jeddah master-builder of the day, it is built of coral limestone tied by teak beams, and contains 50 high-ceilinged rooms, including a famous library of 6,000 volumes.

The character of the town had changed little over the years, prior to 1950. Pilgrims came, and, if they could afford it, went; ships still edged through the dangerous gateways between the three coral reefs; sweet water remained the perennial problem. T. E. Lawrence gave an evocative description of the Jeddah of 1916 in *Seven Pillars of Wisdom*:

> It was indeed a remarkable town. The streets were alleys, wood-roofed in the main bazaar, but elsewhere open to the sky in the little gap between the tops of the lofty white walled houses ... Housefronts were fretted, pierced and pargetted till they looked as though cut out of cardboard for a romantic stage setting.

Above:

Binding the sea to the city was the guiding principle of Jeddah's city planners, under mayor Mohammed Said Farsi, during the city's phenomenal expansion in the 1970s and early 1980s. The corniche road connecting the marine lagoon of down-town Jeddah continues for some 40 km to the north and south of the core of the city, luring the citizen to the landscaped elegance that leads to the beaches and the sea's underwater coral fairyland.

Right:

The waterfront of central Jeddah is dominated by the National Commercial Bank, the splendid, hollowed triangular building which stands in the heart of the commercial district. This section of the city lies just to the north of the port and behind a tranquil lagoon.

The Architectural Heritage of the Western Region

Makkah, Madinah, Ta'if and Jeddah all had a similar type of architecture. Today, traditional houses survive only in Old Jeddah, whose cool and narrow streets and ancient *suq* have been preserved, and are illustrated here. Parts of Taif, too, have been saved from the relentlessness of modernisation.

The buildings once common to all these cities were two, three or more storeys, with flat roofs. The entrances were often vaulted by a round-headed or pointed arch, and the wooden doors decorated with intricate stylized carving. The outer walls were frequently whitewashed. Elaborate fretwork decoration was lavished upon the wooden screens which faced the upper storeys of the building around windows and balconies, echoing the *mashrabiyya* screens of Cairo. These screens, admitting the flow of fresh air, guarded from view those behind windows or on balconies. They were arranged on the façade of the building in various ways, in some houses occupying the whole of the upper area. The upper storeys of some merchants' houses, like Beit al-Turki were given projecting loggia, suspended high above the street by a sequence of cantilevers and projecting corbels.

For Jeddah in particular, and also for the inland cities, coral limestone provided the basic structural material, and has withstood the tests of the century and a half since most surviving houses were erected.

*Beit al-Turki's cantilevered balconies and loggias (**right**) are a monument to the ingenuity of Jeddah's nineteenth-century master craftsmen.*

*Beit Nassif (**left**) is the jewel in the crown of Jeddah's far-sighted preservation of the core of the "old town".*

*The streetlife of Jeddah has always been vibrant, with open air cafés and pavement stalls across the city (**opposite**). An outgoing social community has inherited the cosmopolitan influence of the numerous travellers who have passed through the port – a great many on pilgrimage – over the centuries. The malls, hotels and currency exchanges and banks of the city centre (**above**) benefit from the flow of visitors, who now arrive mostly by air, and from the city's modern port.*

Every storey jutted, every window leaned one way or another; often the very walls sloped ... The atmosphere was oppressive, deadly. There seemed no life in it. It was not burning hot, but held a moisture and sense of great age and exhaustion such as seemed to belong to no other place ... a feeling of long use, of the exhalations of many people, of continued bath-heat and sweat.

The town surrendered to Abdul Aziz and his followers in 1925. But its modern history does not begin until May 1933, when his Finance Minister, Abdullah Sulaiman, signed an oil concession with the Standard Oil Company: £35,000 pounds in gold sovereigns were counted across a table in Jeddah. Five years later oil began to flow in the Eastern Province and Jeddah's days as a walled city were numbered. From 1850 to 1945 the population had been stable at about 25,000: by 1993 it had exceeded 2 million. Such hectic growth

brought formidable challenges for the Mayor and his city planners, as it spread up the coast. To the north and inland along the Makkah road land and property prices spiralled. But the greatest challenge was to the harbour, which had become the country's main gateway for building materials and consumer goods entering in vast quantities.

The King Abdul Aziz International Airport, which covers over 40 square miles, provides for over two million pilgrims (as well as six million other passengers) each year, and is capable of handling 6,000 passengers per hour at its three adjacent terminals. Beside the domestic and international terminals, pilgrims arrive and leave through a special *Hajji* terminal (see pages 156-157), a magnificent open-air structure with 210 tent-like roof units forming the largest fabric roof in the world, which can accommodate 80,000 pilgrims at any one time.

Until the 1920s, Jeddah boasted but a single

tree, still standing at Beit Nassif. Today, desalination having solved the city's water problem, the whole of Jeddah has grown green with some eight million trees, and many areas of waste ground have been transformed into parks. The development of the Corniche as an attractive promenade with trees and innovative sculptural monuments has decisively brought the sea back into the life of the city.

Jeddah is now not only a thriving business and commercial centre but also a resort for citizens and visitors from many parts of the Kingdom, attracted by good shops, hotels, restaurants, and beaches up as far as Obhor Creek twenty miles north of the city, which offer access to the dazzling marine life of the coral reef.

What remained of the coral houses of the old city in the mid 1970s has been conserved. The Abdul Raouf Hasan Khalif Museum recaptures the flavour of life in Jeddah's pre-oil days.

Yanbu

Yanbu, the region's second port, features as Madinah's port on the earliest maps of the Red Sea coast. Since the 1970s it has – with Jubail – been the key to the Kingdom's industrialisation plans to develop hydrocarbon-based and energy intensive industries, and thus reduce the Kingdom's dependence on oil revenues alone. It is the largest petroleum and petrochemical exporting complex in the Red Sea, fed by a gas and oil pipeline from the Eastern Province. Yanbu's resident industries include the liquification of gas, aluminium, ethylene, glycol and polymer.

Ta'if

The attractive city of Ta'if, by virtue of its elevation (1,500 metres), became increasingly the summer resort of those seeking to escape the stifling heat of the low coastland. Today, a similar migration takes place from the east. Monarch, court and cabinet move to Ta'if in summer, making it for these months the second capital.

For centuries Ta'if and its fine surrounding uplands have been the provider of fruit for the Hejaz, and the centre of the production of rosewater.

Right:

The roundabouts of Jeddah encircle a large-scale work of art, often whimsical and witty. The elegant sweep of the city's corniche, meanwhile, is adorned with sculptures of outstanding originality and beauty – including that by Henry Moore (**top**) and "Music" (**bottom**), one of six sculptures produced by a group of Belgian artists following the 1984 Brussels exhibition, "Jeddah, Yesterday and Today". In the background lies the Al Anani Mosque, designed by Raouf Helmi.

Opposite:

The El-Wakil mosque in Jeddah won the Aga Khan Award for Islamic Architecture in 1989.

Eastern Region

The People and their History

The low-lying coastal strip of the Eastern Province has relatively plentiful water and thus has been immemorially populated. It was here that oil was first discovered. The shore is sandy with salt flats (*sabkhas*), occurring in depressions. Sandy plains stretch from Jubail to Kuwait Bay, and drifting sand and dunes from Jubail southward. A great belt of sand known as the Dahna and a rock plateau called the Summan – a grassy prairie after good winter rains – and the great al-Hasa oasis are the region's main interior features. Historically, migrations from Najd into the Eastern Province, and regular communication between the al-Hasa oasis and the tribes and towns of the Riyadh area and southern Najd, ensured a homogeneity of tribal culture. The area was in contact with the cities of Mesopotamia as early as the fifth century BC: Ubaid pottery of the time is found in plenty along the coast. The earliest references to the land of Dilmun, later centred on Bahrain, in the third millenium BC, are taken to refer to the Eastern Province. In the first millennium BC, trade routes from the incense kingdoms of South Arabia emerged in al-Hasa, bringing wealth to towns like the lost city of Gerrha (referred to by Strabo, Pliny and others) and Thaj, now an archaeological site.

The location of Gerrha is yet to be confirmed, following the chance discovery of ancient city foundations at an inland desert site south of Jubail in the late 1990s. From about the third century AD a slump in trade led to a decline in wealth of the coastal towns and coincidentally a growth in the nomadic way of life as tribes migrated into this area from south-west Arabia. Power was increasingly held by tribal confederations, supported for several centuries before Islam by the Sassanids of Persia who exercised control over the area. The Umayyads ruling from Damascus and then the Abbasids ruling from Baghdad controlled the area between the seventh and tenth centuries AD. Successively ruled by the Qarmatians, Uyunids and the Qays, by the fourteenth century al-Hasa and Qatif were flourishing, as commented on by the visiting traveller, Ibn Battuta (*see* p.52). For a time in the

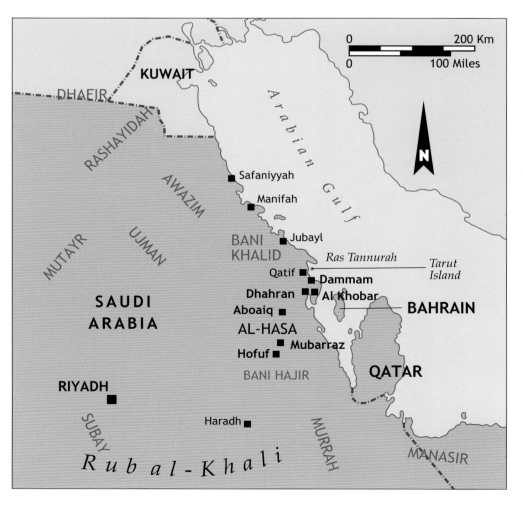

The Arabian Gulf has been the major conduit for trade between the Indus valley to the east, the Nile to the west, and Mesopotamia to the north since the dawn of those civilisations. Along the route, the small communities of settlers living off the sea began to flourish as victuallers and middlemen for the sea-borne traders. Small fishing craft such as the one shown in a shot from the 1950s (*opposite above*) or under repair (*above*) and the booms (*opposite below*) are still used. For the better part of twenty centuries, the coastland and islands flourished upon their production of pearls – until the cultured pearl from the Far East eclipsed the natural product.

Left:
Tribal distribution in Eastern Saudi Arabia.

The demand for labour – skilled and unskilled – generated by the oil industry and the massive industrialism of Jubail has drawn recruits from all the tribes of the hinterland. Through tribal allegiance a territorial kinship still prevails.

fifteenth century the Jabris, a power of local origin, ruled the area but ceded control to the Turks in the sixteenth century. Ottoman rule continued, on and off, until it was overthrown by the al-Saud in 1913.

For many centuries, pearling provided a livelihood for those families of boat owners, divers, and merchants who gave high fashion its natural pearls until the cultured pearls of the Far East snuffed out the industry.

Today the wealth of the region is, of course, oil based: money and people have flooded in. The recent expansion of the complex of towns encompassed by the port city of Dammam, al-Khobar and Dhahran has been phenomenal. A causeway now links the area to Bahrain. Inland, the oil wells, pipelines and infrastructure of the petrochemicals industry pinpoint where industrial man has intruded upon the traditional lands of the tribe. Even so, there is always a "beyond" in Arabia; and beyond this intrusion the nomad does indeed pursue his life. The presence of the Murrah tribe, for example, along the northern edge of the Empty Quarter, is a relic of the Bedouin past, of the severe disciplines of heat (and sometimes cold), aridity, and austere dependence on sparse pasture alleviated by space and the freedom of desert migration. These tribesmen move on in pursuit of grazing for their animals every few days throughout most of the year. They live largely on their animals' milk products and to a lesser extent on their meat, on dates, and on small amounts of rice and unleavened bread. Their inherited independence makes it difficult for them to fit into schemes of modern development. The agriculturalist is generally better fed and better sheltered.

Meanwhile, of course, the oil industry has brought prosperity to the whole province's urban population.

*Oil has remained as the source of education in the Eastern Province. Casoc, the precursor to Saudi Aramco, the company which today manages much of the nation's oil extraction, early shouldered the task of educating the youth from the local community. The state-funded King Fahd University of Petroleum and Minerals (**left, and above**) is a bastion of the education of the nation's youth, preparing fresh generations of Saudi Arabians with the expertise to take over from the expatriate population.*

The Arabian Horse

The legendary Arabian horse originated in the deserts of Saudi Arabia and through the centuries has been highly regarded for its extraordinary stamina and endurance. The Bedouin of the Arabian peninsula, who perfected the breed with unswerving attention over a great many generations, were scrupulous in control of the bloodlines of their horses. The history of every Arab mare was so important to the tribe that the head man knew all the pedigree of each animal as closely as he knew the genealogy of his own family. The horse was seen as a gift from God, created from mist and dust, and a beast to be treated with love and respect, worthy of affection as a member of the family. The gentle temperament of the purebred Arabian horse, and its courage, speed and stamina, are qualities which were vital in attack and escape to the raiding Bedouin, and are today valued in modern studs and on the racecourse.

The Arabian horse stands between fourteen and fifteen hands in height and most commonly are bay, chestnut, or grey. The head is proportionately smaller than that of the English thoroughbred, the chief difference lying in the depth of the jowl and the "dished" profile. The ears are relatively large but beautifully shaped, the eyes large and mild, the forehead wide and prominent, and the muzzle fine, sometimes almost pinched. The crest is slightly arched and the neck strong; the head is held high, the shoulders oblique, and the hoofs are round, large and very hard. The back is short and the croup longer and typically more level, with the tail set higher than in most other saddle breeds; indeed, Arabs have boasted that they could use them to hang their cloaks on.

Every one of today's thoroughbreds is a direct descendant of one of three Arab sires: the Byerley Turk (an Arabian stallion captured from the Turks), the Godolphin Arabian, and the Darley Arabian. For cross-breeding, the Arab stallion is notable for the transmission, to inferior stocks, of constitution, intelligence and heart.

And God took a handful of South Wind
and from it formed a horse, saying:

"I create thee, Oh Arabia. To thy forelock I bind victory in battle.
On thy back I set a rich spoil and a Treasure in thy loins.
I establish thee as one of the Glories of the Earth…
I give thee flight without wings."

From an ancient Bedouin legend

The Towns

Dammam

The port of Dammam, capital of the Eastern Province and the city closest to Dhahran, home of the oil industry, grew so rapidly since the 1970s that it has now all but merged with its neighbours, al-Khobar (once a fishing village whose inhabitants supplemented their living with pearling) and Dhahran (composed of the adjacent compounds of Saudi Aramco and King Fahd University of Petroleum and Minerals) to form a single municipality. The area is now linked to Bahrain by a causeway.

Hofuf

The town of Hofuf – named after the "murmuring" of its streams – is the centre of al-Hasa Oasis, which is one of the largest oases in the world, whose abundant artesian waters have supported settlement since ancient times. Its colonnaded date palms number in the millions. It produces famous dates. Hofuf has one of the oldest mosques in Arabia, the Jawatha Mosque. The Turks ruled this area in the sixteenth century (from which period dates the Mosque of Ibrahim and the Turkish fort, Qasr Ibrahim), and again in the late nineteenth century, until expelled by Abdul Aziz al-Saud in 1913.

Jubail

Jubail, once a minor port and fishing settlement, was chosen with Yanbu on the Red Sea coast in the 1970s to spearhead the Kingdom's new industrialisation programme and diversify output away from a sole dependancy on oil. It is today the site of a wide range of modern manufacturing: steel, aluminium, plastics and fertilisers.

Qatif

The port Qatif, supplied by its abundant inland wells, with its large fort, was won in the 16th century by Ottomans from the Portuguese, who remained for a while on nearby Tarut Island, Qatif, like Hofuf, fell to the al-Saud in 1913.

*The mysterious rocky outcrop of Jabal Qarah (**opposite**) becomes a magnet of weekend attraction for the residents of al-Hasa and Hofuf.*

*The Jabri Mosque in Hofuf (**above**) echoed the regionally characteristic shape of the Rajhiyah mosque in Qatif (**below**).*

The Architectural Heritage of the Eastern Region

The eastern towns of Saudi Arabia are situated between the desert and the Arabian Gulf. The climate is similar to that of the Red Sea shore, with high humidity and unrelenting heat in summer. As on the Red Sea coast, the building material is coral aggregate and wood. The walls are of pier and beam construction with rubble infill, made smooth with plaster. The roofing system employs palm thatch and wooden beams. Although there is no single local form of building, technical and decorative devices such as arches in carved plaster work recur in structures built for many a purpose. All of these eastern buildings are distinguished by fine proportions, both in dimensions and decoration. The wind-towers of Bahrain and Dubai do not appear on the Saudi coast. Instead, on the Saudi shore, certain rooms are arranged to benefit from the slightest breeze, while other rooms are better suited to cooler winter conditions. Thus, in the centre of Qatif, the houses are of several storeys. The lower rooms have small windows, whereas the uppermost storey has large arched openings piercing the walls for ventilation. This eastern architecture bears no significant relationship to buildings inland, but has a marked similarity to those of traditional Bahrain, Qatar and Dubai.

Northern Region

The People and their History

The folk living across the vast territory south of Iraq and Jordan customarily eat twice a day, the main meal in the evening, a diet based on milk and supplemented by bread, coffee, dates and sometimes locusts.

As the various tribes differ in dialect, so do they in dress. They all wear the same basic *thobe*, but of varying colours, cut and ornament.

A single family can manage 40 to 50 camels, but can survive on 15. Summer encampments on the high ground have been known to exceed 10,000 tents.

The sheikh is the head of the tribe, chosen from the leading family for his courage, generosity and mediating skill. Today they deal with the Government over concessions for oil drilling, rents payable for pipelines crossing their grazing, jobs at the new administrative centres and vehicle licensing.

The Towns

Tabuk

Tabuk has grown to be the busiest town, given its position on today's main north-south highway. Its busy main streets take the heavy traffic of container trucks bringing goods overland from Europe to the Kingdom. But Tabuk has an ancient history. There is a Turkish fort, nearly 300 years old, at the edge of the town.

Ha'il

Ha'il, home of the formidable tribe of al-Rashid who at one time ruled over Najd, lies under the Jebel Shammar. To its north is the great Nafud desert. For centuries Ha'il was seen as the "key to the desert", the main transit point for pilgrims heading for Makkah and Madinah and for traders travelling north or south in the Arabian peninsula. Towards the end of the Abbasid Caliphate, Ha'il became an important centre of learning when its scholars took responsibility for protecting and promulgating Arabic in its purest form. It boasts many famous heroes and poets.

Al-Jawf

Al-Jawf is an oasis town of antiquity. Formerly known as Dumat al-Jandal, it is referred to in the Bible. The old town is sited on the slopes of a great basin surrounded by cliffs and is at the southern end of the great Wadi Sirhan through which traders and merchants have passed for centuries. Beside it stands the new town and both are dominated by a great castle, Qasr Mared, on a hill site of ancient settlement. There is archaeological evidence here of the presence of Assyrians and Nabataeans.

Following its conquest by Muslims in the third year of the *Hijra*, al-Jawf became a staging post for Muslim armies setting out to spread the word of Islam. Its mosque, believed to have been founded by Caliph Omar, is possibly the third oldest in Islam, and has an unusually shaped and attractive minaret.

Beyond the crumbling stone walls of the old town, and the white concrete buildings of the new, stretch the palm groves, orchards and meadows of the oasis. As with all oasis towns, dates were long the staple food and all other plants – fruit trees, vegetables, and alfalfa – were cultivated in their shade. In addition al-Jawf produces wheat and its wide variety of fruit and vegetables include grapes, figs, olives, potatoes and tomatoes.

Sakaka

Sakaka, near al-Jawf, is famous for its standing stones, Rajajil ('the men'), thought to date from the fourth millenium BC and lively rock carvings on the Jebel Burnus, an outcrop projecting from the near-vertical rock which is crowned by the Zabal fort.

Tayma

Tayma, an ancient city on the incense routes from south Arabia, has a history dating from at least until the second millennium BC. In the sixth century BC it was the provincial residence of Nabonidus, King of the Babylonians. A remarkable stele, the Tayma stone, now in the Louvre, carries one of the most important Semitic inscriptions ever found. It dates from the fifth century BC and is written in Aramaic.

Opposite:

A view of Al-Jawf showing the mosque of Omar, possibly the third oldest mosque in Islam.

Right:

The fort of Barzan at Ha'il no longer stands, but is shown here in a pen and ink drawing by an unknown traveller during the 1890s.

Southern Region

The People and their History

The Southern Region comprises the high, forested, mountain ranges of the Asir and the coastal plain of the Tihama. Asir, means "the difficult region". As one moves southwards, the range becomes the south-western massif of peaks, terraced valleys and plateaux at over 2,000 metres. The line of hills begins to the north of Ta'if and includes the hill of Arafat, known to all pilgrims to Makkah. The route south through the foothills was difficult until the building of today's highways, one of which follows the crest of the range, and others – masterly feats of engineering when they were built – wind down the mountainside connecting the crest to the Tihama plain some 1,800 metres below. Occasional floods have swept these roads and bridges away, leaving masses of debris, including huge lumps of concrete strewn about the hillside.

This area is the one well-watered region of Saudi Arabia: dependable rains come twice a year, in the north more heavily in the winter and in the south more heavily in the summer, with the monsoon. Thus there is an abundance of trees, such as juniper and wild olive, and settlements with terraced farming. The mountain communities were isolated for centuries. They existed by growing enough to be self-sufficient, on terraces contouring the hillsides which protect the soil from being washed away. The produce of these terraces includes cereals and fruit.

There is a celebrated grace and confidence among the highland people: the women rarely veil themselves, and wear colourful dresses, in some areas with broad-brimmed sombrero-type hats and plenty of jewellery. The different regions are identified according to the tribal groups which inhabit them. The most important groups, from north to south, are Zahran, Ghamid, Bajr, Asir, Shahran, and Qahtan. When referring to a particular area one says, for example, Bilad Zahran, "the land of Zahran", or Bilad Asir, "the land of Asir".

The Tihama is divided into the plain which runs along the coast of the Red Sea (where villages of African-like conical brushwood huts,

*The southwest of Arabia is the peninsula's most fertile region, and also its most mountainous. The highlands of the Asir (**bottom**) enjoy a very different climate from the dryer lowlands of the rest of the country. The traditional architecture in this mountainous region is surprisingly adventurous, with mud brick towers that reach up into the sky, as in the small village of Al Mounis in the Asir (**below**). The Governor of the neighbouring province of Najran had a mud palace built along similar lines (**opposite**).*

*The mountains used once to form a near impassable barrier. Roads have been dauntlessly constructed to open up this mountainous and well-watered quarter of Arabia, like that (**left**) winding up from Jizan to Abha. Some communities are still not easily reached and many continue to enjoy an ancestral way of life and a remoteness (as illustrated **above and overleaf**).*

sometimes surrounded by a reed palisade, can still be seen), and the hilly land behind. Local people include both the settled (the occupants of the brushwood villages) and goat-herderring nomads on the plain and in hills behind. The nomadic people of the hills in the Tihama are mainly of the Qahtani tribe, one of the oldest tribes of Arabia from whom all Saudis of southern Arabia claim descent. They are a good-looking people, hardy mountain dwellers, small of stature, who traditionally wore distinctive head-dresses incorporating herbs and multicoloured woollen headbands. Until modern times the men would often go bare-chested, carrying a sword-like curved dagger just under a metre long, a protection against leopards.

Coastal Tihama is flat and sandy. Agriculture, particularly millet crops, has been boosted by the dams above Jizan and Najran. Fishing is a major local industry, the Spanish mackerel being a principal source of protein food. The traditions of seamanship have maintained links with the Eritrean coast across the Red Sea.

Included in the Southern Region are the islands in the Red Sea, the largest group of which is the Farasan Islands, lying off Jizan. Low-lying and surrounded by coral reefs, they have the distinction of their own species of gazelle.

In both the highlands and the lowlands the many markets constitute an important part of the people's life. The market in a village may be open every day or only once a week. If only once a week, market day is a social occasion for the people of the neighbouring villages. Often the name of the village incorporates the name of the day on which the market was customarily held. Thus: Khamis Mushayt,

143

"the Thursday of Mushayt", Ahad Rufaydah, "the Sunday of Rufaydah". Such places are usually referred to by the people of the region only by the name of their market day: Khamis, Ahad. In some towns, where the market nowadays is open all week, as in Abha and Khamis Mushayt, the original market day sees more wares on display than other days of the week. On market day one may find nomads travelling up from the Tihama to trade with the highlanders. In the markets, in addition to food and modern goods, one finds local products, such as straw baskets and hats, keys and nails made of locally-mined iron, great bunches of herbs and flowers and soft-stone vessels almost identical to those produced in this and other parts of Arabia for millennia.

The Asir was for centuries a warlike region where feuds between villages were commonplace. The disused watchtowers which dot the landscape everywhere are witnesses of that period. Little is known of the early history of the area, but the incense routes from the prosperous south Arabian kingdoms of Yemen passed through Najran, forking to head either north-east via Qaryat al-Fao or north, probably via Tathlith. The region remained relatively undisturbed by the outside world until in the nineteenth century it fell to the Ottoman invaders. The al-Idrisi family ruled the region under the Turks and continued after the Turks had left until Asir and the whole Southern Region was absorbed into the Kingdom of Saudi Arabia in 1934.

The Towns

Abha

Abha, the main town of the Asir region, is home of the regional governorate. Formed by the Ottomans out of the Asiri tribal centre, it is a bustling regional capital, the distinctive architecture of its remaining old houses (*see box on page 149*) now swamped by modern buildings around the old centre. It is situated at 2,200 metres above sea-level and has a moderate climate with the highest rainfall of any town in Arabia. The surrounding mountains are high (Jebel Sawdah is the highest in Arabia), clothed in forests of juniper and wild olive. Out of this beautiful natural environment the Asir National Park has been created and is a significant tourist attraction.

Opposite:

In the agricultural communities of the Asir, children take part in the day-to-day working life of the family – as a straw weaver, say, or goat herd – even as young as this confident little girl.

Below:

An onion-seller at the Najran market protects himself from the sunlight while still wearing thobe *and jacket against the chill of the altitude.*

Khamis Mushayt

Khamis Mushayt ("the Thursday of Mushayt") was originally one of the hill markets to which tribesmen and villagers brought their produce. It is still a lively market and not just on Thursdays, and has grown enormously since the 1980s, partly due to its becoming the site of a military base.

Jizan

Jizan, Saudi Arabia's third most important port on the Red Sea after Jeddah and Yanbu, has a rich agricultural hinterland where coffee, barley, millet, wheat and fruit are grown. It is surrounded by pasture-land and backed by the mountain, Fifa, which reaches 3,400 metres and is part of the Alsarawat range. It has a reservoir dam. At a capacity of 75 million cubic metres it was the largest in the country until the Najran and Wadi Bisha dams were built.

Al-Baha

Al-Baha has in recent years become a popular holiday resort in the Asir mountains for visitors attracted by its equable climate and the surrounding forests.

Najran

Najran, situated on the fertile Wadi Najran east of the Asiri massif, has always been an important entrepôt and a rich agricultural area. The wadi is lined with large, fine old mud-brick farmhouses. In the centre of the town the elegant but dominant former Governor's fort, Qasr al-Nashmi, rises with its pointed white crenellations crowning its many roofs. While Najran remains a provincial capital, the Qasr is a heritage site.

At the time of the lucrative incense trade from the kingdoms of Yemen with the Mediterranean markets, the routes forked at Najran, north or north-east as we have mentioned, the route due north skirting the eastern edge of the Asir mountains. It was once a centre of Himyaritic Christianity.

The ruins of the pre-Islamic city of Ukhdud lie just outside modern Najran with a museum beside them. In the 1970s a substantial dam was built behind the town of Najran, to regulate the flow of rainwater and conserve underground water, for irrigation of crops. With a capacity of 85 million cubic metres, this dam is the second largest in the Kingdom.

The Architectural Heritage of the Southern Region

In southern Hejaz and Asir, from Bilad Zahran and through Bilad Ghamid, north of Abha, the standard building material is rough-cut stone. These villages are often defensively positioned on hilltops, especially in Bilad Zahran, and the contiguous faces presented by the outermost houses give the effect of a fortified wall. Some villages have so many of these high fortified buildings that they resemble skyscrapers as seen *(left)*. Inside the houses, however, it is a much more welcoming picture with walls painted in wide bands of bright primary colour or stylised patterns. In valleys and plains further south, the villages are unfortified. A characteristic of both regions are the rectangular watch towers mounted by an interior spiral stairway. They taper towards the top, which is slightly crenellated, and vary in height and proportion.

As for the Abha area itself, the houses are built of mud or stone or a combination of both, as seen *(above)* in the village of Sarat Adidah, southeast of Abha. In those buildings constructed of mud, layers are applied successively and each layer is left to dry before another is added. Horizontal rows of protruding stone slabs are placed between each mud-layer to break up the flow of rainwater, which would otherwise dissolve the mud. The mud surfaces of the houses are often white-washed, emphasizing the horizontal division of these tower-like structures. Further south, in Najran, the architectural style is more like that of Yemen, as, for example, in the halfmoon shaped windows of tinted glass above the main windows of the house. The mud buildings are crowned with crenellations and white paint outlines the windows.

On the Tihama plain can still be found villages of conical huts of brushwood with elaborately decorated interiors. The influence of Africa is clearly to be seen. The houses are built in clusters behind high reed palisades. Amid the flats inland from Jizan, these villages present remarkable toothed silhouettes against the skyline. Inside, the single-chamber houses, lined with mud, are brilliantly painted with imaginative designs that reach to the pinnacle of the under-roof.

The taste for startlingly bright exterior decoration on houses is unique to the mountain region straddling the Saudi-Yemeni border, and stands in stark contrast with russets and deep greys favoured by the desert-dwellers to the east and north.

The Rub al-Khali

The Rub al-Khali, or Empty Quarter is the Kingdom's fifth region and scant indeed are inhabitants. It stretches across the southern part of the Kingdom from the foothills of the Asir mountains in the west to the borders of the Emirates in the east and of Yemen and Oman in the south.

This vast sandy area has often been described as resembling the sea with its wave-like lines of dunes (*uruq*). It is the largest sand desert in the world. It was not always thus: in earlier geological periods lakes formed and animals roamed the plains, hunted by palaeolithic man and, for some while after the most recent wet period, which commenced about 9000 BC, Neolithic man hunted game and birds and cultivated cereals in settlements beside lakebeds. After the lakes dried up and the dunes covered these settlements, only nomadic Bedouin crossed the sands, using the rare wells. The appeal of the stark beauty of a landscape virtually devoid of vegetation has been vividly described by the explorer Wilfred Thesiger who crossed the eastern part of the desert in the late 1940s with his Bedouin companions:

It is a bitter, desiccated land which knows nothing of gentleness or ease. Yet men have lived there since earliest times. Passing generations have left fire-blackened stones at camping sites, a few faint tracks polished on the gravel plains ... No man can live this life and emerge unchanged ... For this cruel land can cast a spell which no temperate clime can match.

The first Westerners to cross the Empty Quarter were Bertram Thomas and H. St John Philby in the 1930s. Nowadays there are fewer true Bedouin but a larger number of adventurous expatriates roaming the sands, in soft-tyred vehicles designed for the terrain.

Left:
Remarkably, plantlife occasionally manages to seed itself amid the scorched and shifting sands of the Rub al-Khali.

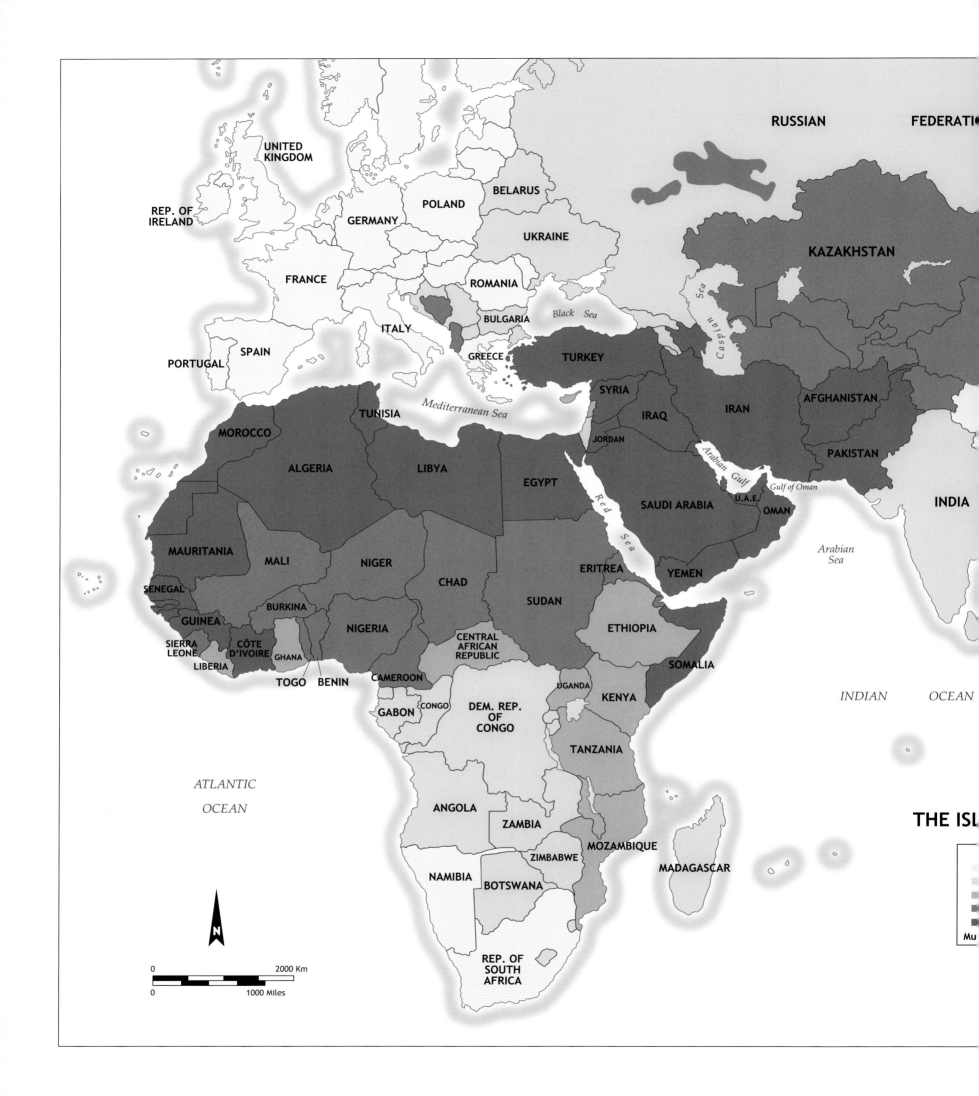

RUSSIAN FEDERATIO

UNITED KINGDOM

REP. OF IRELAND

BELARUS

POLAND

GERMANY

UKRAINE

KAZAKHSTAN

FRANCE

ROMANIA

Black Sea

BULGARIA

Caspian Sea

PORTUGAL

SPAIN

ITALY

GREECE

TURKEY

SYRIA

IRAN

AFGHANISTAN

IRAQ

JORDAN

PAKISTAN

INDIA

TUNISIA

Mediterranean Sea

MOROCCO

ALGERIA

LIBYA

EGYPT

Arabian Gulf

SAUDI ARABIA

U.A.E.

Gulf of Oman

OMAN

Red Sea

MAURITANIA

MALI

NIGER

CHAD

SUDAN

ERITREA

YEMEN

Arabian Sea

SENEGAL

BURKINA

NIGERIA

ETHIOPIA

GUINEA

SIERRA LEONE

CÔTE D'IVOIRE

GHANA

CENTRAL AFRICAN REPUBLIC

SOMALIA

LIBERIA

TOGO BENIN

CAMEROON

UGANDA

KENYA

GABON

CONGO

DEM. REP. OF CONGO

INDIAN OCEAN

TANZANIA

ATLANTIC

OCEAN

ANGOLA

ZAMBIA

MOZAMBIQUE

ZIMBABWE

MADAGASCAR

THE ISL

NAMIBIA

BOTSWANA

N

0   2000 Km

0   1000 Miles

REP. OF SOUTH AFRICA

Mu

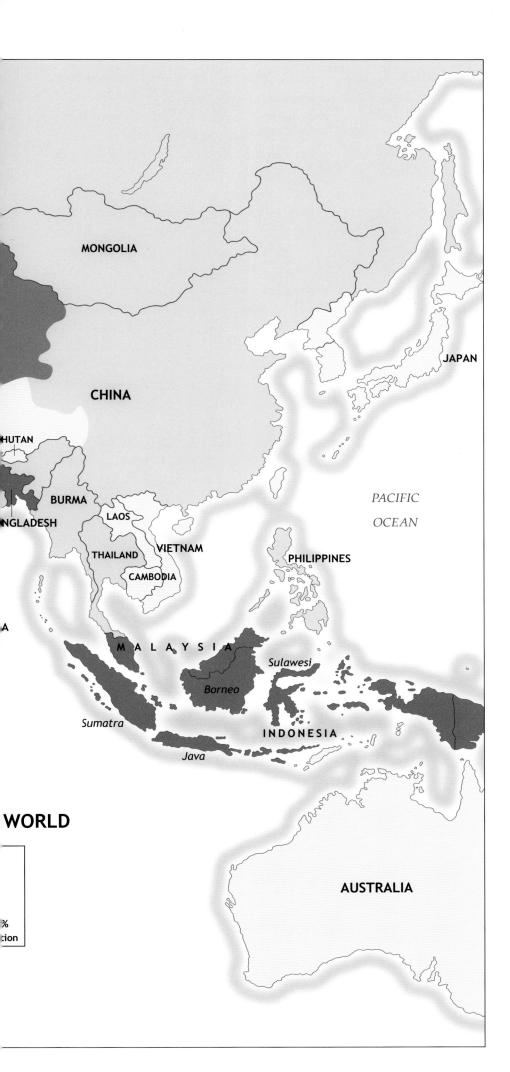

5

Islam

To Saudi Arabia, the holy cities of Makkah and Madinah are a sacred trust, exercised on behalf of all Islam. To the fountainhead of their faith every year flock pilgrims in their millions, to offer their "submission", as is the meaning of Islam, to God's will as revealed through the Prophet Muhammad.

MONGOLIA

JAPAN

CHINA

HUTAN

BURMA

LAOS

NGLADESH

THAILAND   VIETNAM

PHILIPPINES

CAMBODIA

PACIFIC
OCEAN

A

M A L A Y S I A

Sulawesi

Borneo

Sumatra

INDONESIA

Java

AUSTRALIA

WORLD

%
tion

Note: All quotations from the Holy Qur'an are drawn from the Yusuf Ali translation.

THE KINGDOM OF SAUDI ARABIA

Islam is a world-wide faith. There exists today a world Muslim community of about 1.3 billion people which, despite sectarian differences, feels itself clearly bound together in one faith. Every Muslim must recite the profession of faith, "There is no God but Allah, and Muhammad is his Prophet", with awareness of its meaning and full consent from the heart.

The Qur'an repeatedly states that it is "a reminder for the whole world", that differences of tribes and peoples, of tongues and skin-colour, are signs of God's power and mercy, but that real rank in God's sight depends on piety and virtue, and that the Prophet himself was "sent only as a mercy to all mankind". This universal character of the Islamic teaching was also strongly underlined in the Prophet's Farewell Pilgrimage sermon, which declares the religious ideal to be indifferent to racial and other natural differences.

While today, Arabs constitute a mere third of the world Muslim population, the fact remains that Islam's origins lie in an Arab milieu and that it has a clear Arab base. Muslim thinkers have considered this point and given explanations to rationalize it. Thus, Ibn Khaldun holds that the Prophet had to be born in Arabia, whose people were not primitive, yet were close to the natural state of man and therefore possessed of natural manly virtues and minds unencumbered by preconceived notions. Indeed he had to be born among the Makkan tribe of Quraysh, who, once converted to Islam, had the necessary power and prestige to protect and propagate it. It is, of course, historically true that when Makkah joined Islam, the rest of Arabia followed. Shah Walig Allah of Delhi adds that it was part of the divine plan to replace the older Middle Eastern civilizations with a new civilization which would have a moral freshness and virility that could be supplied only by the Arabs, once they had been nurtured by Islam. Be that as it may, there was undoubtedly a religious ferment in Makkah and al-Madinah prior to the appearance of the Prophet. While the Jews of al-Madinah longed for a Prophet to make them victorious over the Arabs there (Qur'an

II, 83), Arab intellectuals in Makkah, having accepted neither Judaism nor Christianity, desired a new Arab Prophet so that "they may be better guided" than the Jewish and Christian communities (Qur'an XXXV, 42; VI, 157; XXXVII, 168). When the Makkans opposed the Prophet, the Qur'an repeatedly reminded them that he had been raised up "from among themselves" and that they knew him well because he had lived among them for so long. Even more emphatically, the Qur'an time and time again states that it is revealed in a "clear Arabic tongue" (Qur'an XVI, 103; XXVI, 195; also XII, 2; XIII, 37; XX, 113), for "if we had made it a non-Arab Qur'an, they (the opponents) would have said, 'Why are its verses not clearly set out?'" (Qur'an XLI, 44). This last statement refers to the belief of the Arabs that the Arabic language is the most expressive and eloquent.

That the Prophet, since he was an Arab himself, should communicate to his people in Arabic, and that they should be the first addressees of Islam, was, of course, natural. But the statements of the Qur'an about its own nature go much further, since it regards itself as miraculous and challenges its opponents – those Arabs who were proud of their literary perfection - to produce anything like it (Qur'an X, 38; XI, 13; XXVIII, 49). In these verses, the Qur'an emphasizes that its source is divine, and cannot be the composition of a human mind, even that of the Prophet himself. It is clear from accounts of the time that Muhammad's speech, outside of revelation, was indeed of a different quality from that of the Qur'an. Muslim theologians early deduced the doctrine that the Qur'an is "inimitable" and this in itself is seen as proof that the words are heaven-sent. As such, the Qur'an is untranslatable, and renderings of it in English generally refer to it as an "interpretation" rather than a translation. To truly understand the Qur'an's message, Muslims need a grasp of Arabic.

The second major source of Islamic doctrine and practice - particularly in the field of law (shari'ah), which stands at the centre of the entire Islamic system - is the sunnah ("example" or "model") of the Prophet - that is his precepts and conduct, both in private and

public activity. The sunnah interprets and elaborates the teaching of the Qur'an, and is embodied in certain authoritative works. These do not only include what the Prophet actually said or did. At a very early stage, the Muslim jurists decided that the entire body of Arab practices and customs to which the Prophet had not explicitly objected and hence had tacitly approved, is part of the Prophetic sunnah. This concept of the "tacit (sukuti) sunnah" thus sanctified the entire gamut of Arab life - essentially Makkan and Madinan after its reform by the Qur'an and the Prophet. In its outward expansion and during its long development it was certainly modified, elaborated and changed (on the basis of the principle of ijtihad, or "fresh thinking"), but it always served as the normative base of reference.

Besides being the birthplace of Islam, Makkah is the object of the great annual pilgrimage (hajj) undertaken by Muslims to the Ka'abah Sanctuary (the haram), also called the "House of God" (bayt Allah). A pre-Islamic Arab site, it was officially adopted by Islam in the year 1 AH (or AD 622), after reforms purging it of idolatrous practices and implications. It is, for all Muslims, the most holy place, where the divine comes into special touch with the earth. Muslim mystics (Sufis) in particular developed a mystique of the Ka'abah, regarding it as the earthly manifestation of a metaphysical divine reality. Throughout the centuries, almost every Muslim, no matter how distant his abode, has aspired to visit Makkah, rendering it the metropolis of Islam, and the hajj the greatest living religious epic on earth. Scholars and saints - side by side with common folk - have usually visited Makkah, often more than once in their lifetime, to meet scholars and spiritual leaders from other parts of the Muslim world. Many stayed on in Makkah for study, reflection and spiritual enlightenment, some earning the honorific name "Allah's neighbour" (jar Allah). Ibn Arabi (died 1240) of Spain, perhaps the greatest name in Muslim mysticism, entitled his magnum opus, which he wrote at Makkah, "Makkan Illumination" (Futuhat Makkiyah).

The number of pilgrims visiting the holy land annually has risen from an estimated 100,000 in 1925 to around twelve million today. Of these, the majority come for umrah *through the course of the year, still leaving three million who come at the same time specifically for the* hajj. *A large portion come through Jeddah International Airport (**pictured above and right**). Illustrated (**below**) is the sea of humanity, dressed uniformly in the white* ihram *robing and on their way down from Mount Arafat (**left**) to the plain below.*

The *Hajj*

The hajj *terminals* (**left and below**) *outside King Abdulaziz International Airport in Jeddah are the first sight of the heartland for many pilgrims coming on pilgrimage. Their award-winning design makes use of a traditional Arabian tent theme to express welcome and provide shelter for visitors.* (**far right**) *A Muslim leads a group in prayer on arrival at the terminals.*

Overleaf:

The Grand Mosque in Makkah has been subject to wholesale renovation and extension since the 1990s. It is today larger than the entire city at the time of the Prophet.

"For Hajj are the months well known. If any one undertakes that duty therein, Let there be no obscenity, nor wickedness, nor wrangling in the Hajj. And whatever good ye do, (be sure) Allah knoweth it. And take a provision (with you) for the journey, but the best of provisions is right conduct. So fear Me, O ye that are wise."

Verse 197, Surat Al-Baqarah

"And proclaim the Pilgrimage among men: they will come to thee on foot and (mounted) on every kind of camel, lean on account of journeys through deep and distant mountain highways."

Verse 27, Surat Al-Hajj

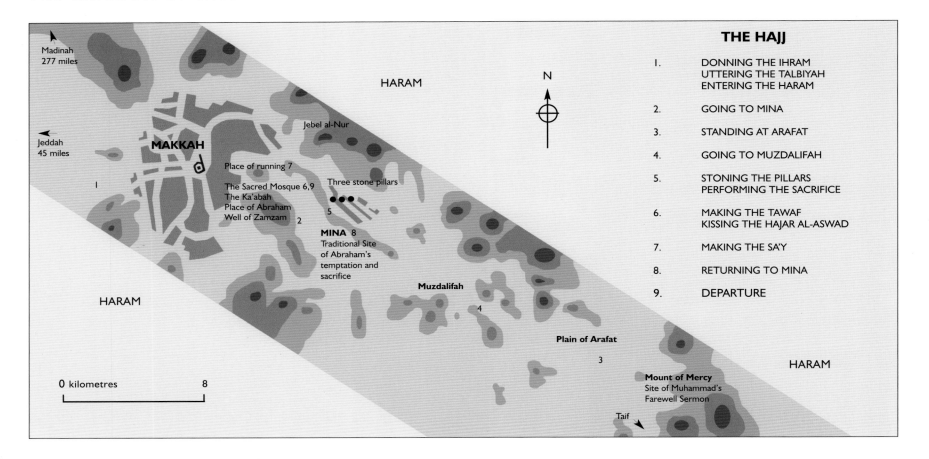

THE HAJJ

1. DONNING THE IHRAM
   UTTERING THE TALBIYAH
   ENTERING THE HARAM

2. GOING TO MINA

3. STANDING AT ARAFAT

4. GOING TO MUZDALIFAH

5. STONING THE PILLARS
   PERFORMING THE SACRIFICE

6. MAKING THE TAWAF
   KISSING THE HAJAR AL-ASWAD

7. MAKING THE SA'Y

8. RETURNING TO MINA

9. DEPARTURE

The Holy Qur'an on the *Hajj*

After belief in the one God (Allah), the performance of regular, ritual prayers, fasting during the month of Ramadan and the giving of fixed alms (*zakat*), the *hajj* is the fifth pillar of Islam, a fundamental duty which a Muslim, male and female alike, must perform at least once in a lifetime if he or she has the material means to do so. Long before the Prophet Muhammad began to preach Islam and summon the Arabs and all mankind back to the worship of the One True God, indeed since time immemorial, the barren valley of Makkah had been a place of pilgrimage venerated by the Arabs, both settled and nomadic. It had been associated with the Patriarch Abraham, the Friend of God, who was the first to establish there a house to the glory of God. In the Holy Qur'an (II, 127-129) we read:

And remember Abraham and Isma'il raised the foundations of the House (with this prayer): "Our Lord! Accept (this service) from us: For Thou art the All-Hearing, the All-knowing.
Our Lord! make of us Muslims, bowing to Thy (Will), and of our progeny a people

Muslim, bowing to Thy (will); and show us our place for the celebration of (due) rites; and turn unto us (in Mercy); for Thou art the Oft-Returning, Most Merciful.

Our Lord! send amongst them a Messenger of their own, who shall rehearse Thy Signs to them and instruct them in scripture and wisdom, and sanctify them: For Thou art the Exalted in Might, the Wise.

Again we read (III, 96-97):

The first House (of worship) appointed for men was that at Bakka: Full of blessing and of guidance for all kinds of beings:

In it are Signs Manifest; (for example), the Station of Abraham; whoever enters it attains security; Pilgrimage thereto is a duty men owe to Allah, those who can afford the journey; but if any deny faith, Allah stands not in need of any of His creatures.

And so the ancient pilgrimage to Makkah became incorporated in Islam; the guiding lines of its performance were laid down by the Holy Qur'an (II, 196 - 7):

And complete the Hajj or Umra in the service of Allah. But if ye are prevented (from completing it), send an offering for sacrifice, such as ye may find, and do not shave your heads until the offering reaches the place of sacrifice. And if any of you is ill, or has an ailment in his scalp, (necessitating shaving), (he should) in compensation either fast, or feed the poor, or offer sacrifice; and when ye are in peaceful conditions (again), if any one wishes to continue the Umra on to the Hajj, he must make an offering, such as he can afford, but if he cannot afford it, he should fast three days during the Hajj and seven days on his return, making ten days in all. This is for those whose household is not in (the precincts of) the Sacred Mosque. And fear Allah, and know that Allah is strict in punishment.

For Hajj are the months well known. If any one undertakes that duty therein, let there be no obscenity, nor wickedness, nor wrangling in the Hajj. And whatever good ye do, (be sure) Allah knoweth it. And take a provision (with you) for the journey, but the best of provisions is right conduct. So fear Me, O ye that are wise.

The *Hajj* Journey

The pilgrimage is made to Makkah, the most sacred city of Islam, where the Prophet Muhammad was born, where his mission was first revealed to him and where he began preaching Islam. In the centre of Makkah stands the Sacred Mosque (*al-Masjid al-Haram*), a large open courtyard enclosed by cloisters, rebuilt and enlarged many times. Roughly in the centre of the Sacred Mosque stands the Ka'abah, the House of God, towards which all Muslims turn their faces in their daily prayers, no matter where they may be. The Ka'abah, as its name denotes, is a cube-shaped building of stone, the front (north-east) and back (south-west) sides being 40 feet long, the other sides being 35 feet and the height fifty feet.

In the east corner, about four feet above ground level, is set the Black Stone in a silver frame. This stone (eight inches in diameter) is believed to be the only remnant of the first mosque built by Abraham and to go back even before him to the time of Adam. The Ka'abah has been rebuilt many times in the course of

Below:

The Ka'abah was a place of pilgrimage long before Islam, but was, with the coming of Islam, declared a solely Muslim shrine, and is the fulcrum of the hajj *pilgrimage. The gold-embroidered black material that clothes the Ka'abah is renewed each year; originally an annual gift from Egypt, it is now meticulously prepared and embroidered in the Kingdom.*

> *"Behold! In the creation of the heavens and the earth, and the alternation of night and day, there are indeed signs for men of understanding, Men who celebrate the praises of Allah, standing, sitting, and lying down on their sides, and contemplate the (wonders of) creation in the heavens and the earth, (with the thought): 'Our Lord! not for naught hast Thou created (all) this! Glory to Thee! Give us salvation from the penalty of the Fire.'"*
>
> **Qur'an III, 191-2**

the centuries, once in the lifetime of the Prophet, before his mission, when he was chosen by chance to place the Black Stone in its position. In the north-east wall of the Ka'abah close to the corner in which the Black Stone is set and some seven feet above the ground is the door to the Ka'abah which is opened at special times. There is nothing inside the building, which was cleansed of its idols when the Prophet returned in triumph to Makkah early in 630. The Ka'abah is covered with a black pall decorated with verses from the Qur'an. This is the *kiswah* (garment) which from the Middle Ages was made in Cairo and brought ceremoniously to Makkah every year by the Egyptian pilgrims. It is now made by local craftsmen.

The two remaining shrines inside the Sacred Mosque are the Station of Abraham (facing the door) where the Patriarch bowed down in prayer and the Well of Zamzam, north-east of the Ka'abah, which sprang up when Hagar was desperately seeking water for the infant Isma'il. Just outside the Sacred Mosque is the *mas'a* (running place) between the rocky hillocks of

al-Safa and al-Marwah, a distance of 440 yards. The *mas'a*, which was until recently an ordinary street with shops, is now covered over and paved with marble flags. It was between these two hills that Hagar ran distractedly seeking water.

Pilgrimage to Makkah is of two kinds. There is the *umrah*, the "lesser pilgrimage" or "visit", which can be performed at any time of the year and is confined to worship at the places mentioned above. Then there is the *hajj* proper, which combines the rites of the *umrah* with others outside Makkah and takes place only once a year in the first part of the month of Dhu 'l-Hijjah, the last month of the Islamic lunar calendar.

Again, the *hajj* and the *umrah* can be performed together (*qiran*) or separately (*tamattu*). The latter is chosen by pilgrims who arrive in Makkah some days before the ninth of the month, which day is the culmination of the pilgrimage. *Tamattu* entails either sacrifice at Mina or fasting during the pilgrimage and on return home.

Nowadays, with frequent and easy means of

The rite of sa'y *is one of the key components of a* umrah *pilgrimage and the pilgrim runs between al-Safa and al-Marwah (**above**). For some pilgrims there will be times of cloistered reading and contemplation (**opposite**).*

The throng of pilgrims leaving the Grand Mosque during Hajj *is immense* (**opposite**). *Once they have reached Mina, the pilgrim brings out the pebbles collected earlier at Muzdalifah* (**above**) *and uses them to stone the pillar of Jamrat al-Aqabab* (**below**).

"It is He Who has made the sea subject, that ye may eat thereof flesh that is fresh and tender, and that ye may extract therefrom ornaments to wear; and thou seest the ships therein that plough the waves, that ye may seek (thus) of the bounty of Allah and that ye may be grateful.

And He has set up on the earth mountains standing firm, lest it should shake with you; and rivers and roads; that ye may guide yourselves;

And marks and sign-posts; and by the stars (men) guide themselves."

Qur'an Sura 16, Verses 14 - 16

"…And when ye are told to rise up, rise up: Allah will raise up, to (suitable) ranks (and degrees), those of you who believe and who have been granted (mystic) Knowledge. And Allah is well-acquainted with all ye do."

Qur'an LVIII verse 11.

transport, the number of pilgrims to Makkah during the pilgrimage month is very large, and commonly exceeds three million.

Most foreign pilgrims arrive either by air or by sea through Jeddah, the nearest port to Makkah, and there the Government has a special *hajj* Administration. From Jeddah they go by bus to Makkah (some fifty miles away), each group of pilgrims being assigned according to their rites (Hanafi, Shafi'i, Maliki, and so on) to a *mutawwif* in Makkah. A *mutawwif* is a special guide and mentor whose duty it is to see that the pilgrims under his wing perform the rites of the pilgrimage correctly, have no difficulties while in the Holy Land and return to their homelands happy and satisfied, having gained the blessing of the pilgrimage properly performed. Each *mutawwif* has under him a number of assistants whose duty it is to accompany groups of pilgrims. Of course, a pilgrim who knows the language and is familiar with Makkah can do without a *mutawwif*, relying on one of the many guides to the *hajj* printed in Arabic or other languages.

Before entering the sacred territory around Makkah - indeed, sometimes from the start of his journey - the pilgrim puts himself in a state of sanctity by ablution, prayer and donning the pilgrim's dress (*ihram*), which for a man consists of two unsewn towels, one worn wrapped around the lower part of the body, the other thrown over the upper part, and unsewn sandals. There is no special dress for a woman except that her face must remain unveiled, no matter what her local customs may be. The reason for these regulations is to emphasize the equality of all pilgrims, high and low, before God.

On and off during his journey and until he enters Makkah the pilgrim chants a short formula of acceptance of the pilgrimage duties (the *talbiyah*). This is: "Here I am in answer to thy call, O God, here I am! Here I am! Thou hast no associate! Here I am! All Praise and Favour and Kingship are thine! Thou hast no associate!"

The rites of the *umrah* are *tawaf* (circumambulation of the Ka'abah), *sa'y* (running between al-Safa and al-Marwah) and

shaving of the head or clipping of the hair. On arrival in Makkah the pilgrim performs *wudu* (ablution before prayer) and goes straight away to the Sacred Mosque which he enters preferably by the Bab al-Salam (Gate of Peace). Around the Ka'abah is a paved area (the *mataf*) on which the pilgrim performs his *tawaf*, beginning at the Black Stone and going around the Ka'abah seven times in an anti-clockwise direction. The pilgrim makes the first three rounds of the Ka'abah at a fast pace and the remainder at walking pace, all the while glorifying God and supplicating His favour and mercy in set phrases generally repeated after his guide. As the pilgrim passes the Black Stone he either kisses it, or touches it or simply makes a motion of his hand towards it. As the throng making *tawaf* is generally very large the last is by far the most common. A policeman is posted on either side of the Black Stone to keep the pilgrims on the move. It is a remarkable fact that the *mataf* is never free from pilgrims, night or day, except at the times of congregational prayer. Muslims in no way worship the Black Stone. They kiss or touch it

because it is known that the Prophet Muhammad did so and thereby they establish a physical link between themselves and the Prophet. And he did so because it was a link between himself and Abraham. *Tawaf* is the first and last religious act of the pilgrim to Makkah.

After performing his *tawaf* the pilgrim then proceeds to the Station of Abraham and there performs two cycles of individual prayer. Before going out from the Sacred Mosque to the *mas'a* he may drink some water from the Well of Zamzam. This water is slightly brackish but is drunk in large quantities by the pilgrims, who often fill their water bottles with it to take home.

The second rite of the *umrah* is *sa'y* (running) between al-Safa and al-Marwah. For this the pilgrim leaves the Mosque by the Bab al-Safa (Safa Gate) and mounts the rocky hillock of that name. After a short prayer he proceeds at walking pace towards the second hillock, al-Marwah, all the while saying prayers and supplications. The second fifth of the distance between the two hillocks, between two marker posts, is covered at a fast pace.

Having performed the *sa'y* between the two hillocks seven times the pilgrim ends up at al-Marwah where he has his head shaved or, more commonly nowadays, his hair cut, which is the third rite of the *umrah*. With this he has completed the *umrah*, and if he has come before the ninth of the month with the intention of separating his *hajj* from *umrah* (*tamattu*), he is now free to put off his *ihram* dress, have a bath and put on his ordinary clothes, entering into the social life of Makkah. If on the other hand, his intention was that his *hajj* and *umrah* should be joined (*qiran*), then he remains in *ihram*.

On the eighth of the month of Dhu'l Hijjah the pilgrims prepare for the culmination of the pilgrimage to Makkah. Those who have performed the *umrah* separately bathe and put on their *ihram* dress again and go to the Mosque to perform *tawaf*. Then the whole mass of the pilgrims and even inhabitants of Makkah move to Mina, four miles away, arriving for noon prayers. Mina is a remarkable place: for five or six days of the pilgrimage

Opposite and below:

The hajj *is in many ways the great social equaliser, bringing together the prince and the pauper, people united in their millions from the four corners of the globe to kneel in worship together. The crowd of over one million people entirely fills the Grand Mosque in Makkah and spills over into the surrounding areas.*

month it is thronged. For the rest of the year it is a ghost town.

Later, on the eighth or early on the ninth of the month, the pilgrims move to the Plain of Arafat, some thirteen miles south-east of Makkah and outside the sacred territory, where the *mutawwifs* have set up their thousands of tents, each with its distinctive flag, arranged in streets. On the morning of the ninth of Dhu'l-Hijjah the pilgrims move about freely, talking with other pilgrims and making new friends from many distant lands. Noon and afternoon prayers are combined at mid-day and the Imam gives a short sermon from the pulpit of Namirah Mosque on the Jabal al-Rahmah (Mount of Mercy), a distinguished landmark of Arafat, on which the Prophet gave his Farewell Sermon in which he summarized the duties of a Muslim.

The whole of the afternoon of the ninth is spent in prayer on the Plain of Arafat. This is the *wuquf* (standing), which is the culmination and cornerstone of the pilgrimage to Makkah. Whoever misses it cannot be said to have performed the pilgrimage. In *wuquf* the pilgrim stands bare-headed all the afternoon in the open air glorifying God, reading the Qur'an and crying aloud "*Labbayka llahumma labbayka*" (Here I am, O God, here I am!). The infirm may sit or seek shade during their devotions but it is considered more meritorious to remain standing all the time.

As soon as the sun sets the whole immense throng gets on the move, making for Muzdalifah, an open plain about half way between Arafat and Mina. There the pilgrims

The Prophet's Mosque in Madinah, from its gilded cupolas (**left**) supported on numerous pillars that create the vast space within (**right**) was also the subject of extensive renovation work at the same time as the Grand Mosque in Makkah. While a visit to the Prophet's Mosque is not specifically a part of the hajj, a great many Muslims include it in their tour.

say their sunset and night prayers combined. Controlling the movement of some three million human beings, in all forms of transport, is a supreme feat of administration by the Saudi police. The pilgrim spends the night under the stars at Muzdalifah and gathers 70 pebbles, each about the size of a chick-pea. Early the next morning (the tenth) after prayer he proceeds to Mina, where the pilgrimage is concluded.

In Mina are three stone pillars surrounded by low walls called *jamrahs*. At the one nearest Makkah (Jamrat al-Aqabab), on the morning of the tenth day, the pilgrim casts seven of his pebbles calling out each time "*Allahu Akbar*" (God is most Great). This is symbolic of man's casting out evil from himself. Then, if necessary, the animals are sacrificed and some of the meat given to the poor. The pilgrims must then return to Mina, for it is there that the pilgrimage ends. With a final shaving of his head or symbolic clipping of his hair the pilgrim emerges from the state of *ihram* and his pilgrimage is concluded. He bathes, puts on new clothes and looks forward to returning

to his home a "*hajj*" or "*hajji*". He must, however, spend the two or three days after the tenth day of Dhu'l-Hijjah in Mina, cast his remaining 63 pebbles at all three *jamrahs*, and perform *tawaf al-ifadah*.

Having completed his pilgrimage the pilgrim is generally eager to be on his way, but there are many who linger in Makkah for days, weeks or even months, some for the rest of their lives. Delay also arises from the difficulty of arranging transport for such a vast multitude. When the day of his departure is fixed the pilgrim goes to the Sacred Mosque for the last time and performs a final *tawaf* (*tawaf al-wida* or *tawaf* of Farewell). He leaves the House of God walking backwards all the time, praising and thanking God and praying that this may not be the last time he enjoys the grace and favour of visiting His Holy House and goes out from the Sacred Mosque by the Bab al-Wida (Gate of Farewell). Then with joyful heart he sets off on his journey home.

But since it is vouchsafed to the vast majority of Muslims to make the pilgrimage to Makkah only once in their lifetimes most

pilgrims combine their pilgrimage with a visit to al-Madinah, sometimes before, but generally after the pilgrimage. There they visit the Prophet's tomb and those of the early Caliphs in the Sacred Mosque. They usually spend several days in this second city of Islam, the city to which the Prophet Muhammad fled from persecution in his native city, where he established the Islamic State and where he lies buried with so many of his noble companions.

The pilgrimage to Makkah used to be an arduous and often perilous adventure, but today it is done in comparative comfort and perfect safety. Nevertheless, owing to the vast numbers of pilgrims, it is still a challenging enterprise, especially when the pilgrimage season falls in the summer months. Yet, when the *hajji* is safe at home with his family and when the month of the *hajj* comes round again he feels that there is nowhere he would rather be than with countless thousands from all corners of the earth thronging the Sacred Mosque and the streets of Makkah, or standing in prayer on the Plain of Arafat.

Left:
The hajji *uses his time in the Holy places for a further spiritual voyage; a time for reading the Qur'an and for contemplation.*

Islam

It is the duty of all Muslims to study and understand the Qur'an. Also it is a source of pride to learn the Qur'an by heart. Islamic studies feature in the curricula of all state schools in Saudi Arabia and all Arabic-medium private schools and Saudi children also participate with pride in a number of regular Qur'an recitation competitions.

Islam stresses the acquisition of knowledge and education. It also regards all people as equal in the eyes of God – which is not to say identical: equal in the sense that they come into this world free from sin and with no material possessions and that they will take nothing material with them when they die; non-identical in that they each have their own separate talents and skills. Islam encourages respect for others, particularly for women and the elderly.

From the personal greeting of *assalaam aleykum* (Peace be Upon You) to the welcome of a newborn infant or the utterances of condolence expressed at the time of death, the formularies of the Faith occur throughout daily life. Each act of formal speech is prefaced with the words which open the Qur'an, *Bismillah ar-Rahmani ar-Rahim* – "in the name of God, the Compassionate, the Merciful". Every promise or expectation will be prefaced by the words *Inshallah*, "God willing" – since one should ever remind oneself that everything that comes to pass does so only subject to the will of Allah. Islam gives thanks for God's gift of free will, and encourages the exercise of that will through work and personal dedication.

The religious duties of the Muslim are premised upon what are known as the Five Pillars of Islam:

- The *shahadatayn* or "Oral Confession": "There is no god but God, and Muhammad is his Prophet"

- The duty to pray five times a day: at dawn, midday, noon, afternoon, sunset and before retiring for the night

- The requirement to fast during the holy month of Ramadan

- The duty to offer *zakat* or alms to the poor, to the value of 2.5 per cent of surplus income

- The duty for each person to try and perform the *hajj* at least once during their lifetime.

The call to prayer echoes out from minarets across the nation's many mosques at each prayer time. In the towns and cities, its mounting call can be heard from every side, the voices of the muezzin varying in tone and clarity, each with the same words, beginning: *Allahu Akbar, Allahu Akbar, Ash-hadu an la illah ila Allah; Muhammad Rasoul Allah:* "God is Great, God is Great, There is no god but God, and Muhammad is his Prophet". Whether the muezzin climbs the steps to the minaret to make the call, or remains at the base to broadcast the call through microphones, it is ensured that the call is heard by the Faithful everywhere.

*The Qur'an is, very literally, the word of God; Muhammad was simply the mouthpiece; the Arabic words used are sacred. It is because of this that the physical book that holds the words of the revelation is endowed with holy significance, an object of reverence that became a focus of fine art in the illuminated manuscripts such as this example from the Abbasid period (**below left**), and the subject of careful reading from an early age (**below right**).*

6

Industry and Development

Oil and gas are key to Saudi Arabia's economy. The hydrocarbon reserves and their derivatives generate more than ninety per cent of the country's wealth. It has been the government's goal to increase the revenue from other sources, decreasing dependence on hydrocarbons. This policy has brought many new products on stream – manufacturing benefiting from the cheap energy provided by the cardinal resources.

The gargantuan scale of Saudi Arabia's refineries (such as the installations along the shoreline at Al-Jubail, shown here) could never have been imagined by the first oil explorers less than a century ago. As the world's principal source of the "black gold", these refineries are of crucial significance to the stability of the world economy.

Economic Overview

Saudi Arabia lies at the very heart of the Middle East, its borders touching no fewer than eight countries. To the north are Jordan, Iraq and Kuwait. Eastward lie the United Arab Emirates, Bahrain and Qatar, and to the south, Oman and Yemen. It is the second-largest oil-producing country in the world, and occupies more than 80 per cent of the Arabian peninsula. It could not, therefore, be anything other than the economic power-house of the region.

Ever since this desert Kingdom became transformed from a romantic land of independent sheikhs, warriors and camels into a modern nation state in the 1930s, oil has driven change. In 1946, when oil revenues reached $10 million per annum, the Kingdom began an extensive programme of nation building that was to involve modern systems of transport and communications, housing, industry, utilities, social services and educational facilities. The sharp oil price increase of 1973 led to the creation of a world-class petrochemical industry, and huge infrastructural development.

By 1977, Saudi Arabia was second only to the then West Germany in monetary reserves, and up until the oil price slump of 1986 it was able to balance its budget and avoid a foreign deficit. Meanwhile formidable expenditure was committed in a series of Five Year Plans, implemented to oversee the country's process of development. The First Plan covered the years 1970-1975, and the Eighth Plan was in train in 2005. Each plan has attempted, with varying success, to make good use of the huge revenues that pour into the country to execute a programme of development while preserving the social balance and values of traditional Saudi life.

Up until the end of the Third Five Year Plan in 1985, the story of Saudi Arabia's economy was fairly simple: oil money came in, and the various Government Ministries set about spending it, without much financial constraint. In fact, ministers were praised for spending as much as possible and coming up with new projects. In theory, everything could be achieved at once, and there was much to be done. In practice, however, the action of pumping huge sums of money into a relatively undeveloped economy caused inflation, social upheaval and numerous bottlenecks. Inflation soared rapidly as the new money chased goods and services which the economy could not supply. Imports and distribution could not meet demand. Queues of ships waited outside the ports of Jeddah and Dammam for several weeks and even months. The ports had too few berths to deal with the supply of goods flooding in from outside. Saudi Arabia had became a virtual Eldorado for European, American and Japanese exporters, themselves suffering from a recession. They came bearing everything from construction materials, electrical generators and manufacturing equipment to cameras, soft furnishings and luxury foods. Saudi Arabians could choose from the best, in an atmosphere of intense competition.

Political pressures soon emerged among young Saudis hungry for more change on the one hand, and on the other, among older and

*The PSRC refinery at Al-Jubail Industrial City (**opposite**, with administration buildings in the foreground) is a joint venture between Shell and Petromin, the Saudi Arabian government agency formed to engage in all phases of the oil and mineral industries as well as industrial development. The oil-driven economy supports a burgeoning population, for whom retail banking (**right**, **top** and **bottom**) is a growth sector, along with other service industries.*

more cautious voices who demanded greater restraint, and feared that the structure of the country could fracture amid such dramatic changes in expectations, living conditions, and indeed in the whole psychology of the country. By 1978, through a series of tough measures, the Government regained control of the administrative and economic situation. From then on, inflation was mastered and a sustainable rate of change became the paramount fiscal aim of the Minister of Finance.

From 1986, with the drop in the oil price and economic slowdown, coinciding with the completion of the majority of the infrastructural projects, the development plans took a new direction. The Government began laying the foundations for a mature, sustainable economy with new priorities: education and training, low-cost energy and raw materials, and a favourable financial climate which would enable the private sector to flourish and become the new engine of the economy. The Saudi Arabia Stock Market had been established in 1984, in order to stimulate the injection of private capital into what had hitherto been a state-led process of development. By 1988 the stock market was experiencing a boom, and in 1990, the Saudi Arabian Monetary Agency (SAMA), the Kingdom's central bank, introduced the Electronic Securities Information System, which launched terminals across the Kingdom, bringing share price information to all. Seven years later, SAMA approved the participation of international investors in the Saudi Stock Market, through mutual funds.

Both state and private sectors were encouraged to diversify away from oil and raw material production into other sectors such as technology, manufacturing and agriculture. In August 1999, a Royal Decree announced the formation of the Supreme Economic Council – prompted, it was declared, by the need to involve a circle of wise contributors in Saudi Arabia's economic policy-making. The 11-member Council has continued to uphold the economic policies of the Kingdom. These are stated as social welfare, the concept of a free economy and a free market for capital, goods, services and products. The Council is working towards the following goals:

• the welfare of society
• the provision of jobs and the optimum use of manpower
• the control of public debt within secure and reasonable limits
• the fair distribution of national income and opportunities for investment and labour
• the diversification of the economic base
• the development of savings and frameworks for safe investment
• the increase of the income of the state and linking it with the movement and growth of the national economy
• the increase of investment of domestic capital and savings in the national economy
• the increase of the contribution of the private sector, and the expansion of its contribution to the national economy
• the enhancement of the ability of the national economy to cope efficiently with international economic changes.

One of the keys to progress and the successful diversification of the country's oil-based economy has been the unleashing of the private sector. Through the Supreme Economic Council, the Government has achieved this with a combination of liberalising the country's trade regime, encouraging foreign investors, and – perhaps most significantly – through privatisation. Since 1997, the Kingdom has been putting in place the regulations and structures with which to enable the privatisation of certain sectors such as telecommunications, railways, education, civil aviation, highway management, sports clubs, municipal services, public parks, waste disposal, water desalination and power generation. The key aim has been to make private ownership of these sectors as widespread as possible among Saudi nationals, and since the turn of the new century, there has been visible progress. The first IPO (Initial Public Offering), launched in December 2002, was a huge success (*see* Telecommunications section). In 2002 the Government also approved the transfer of responsibilities of the state-run postal services from the Ministry of Posts, Telegraphs and Telephones to the private sector, and in January 2003, the Director-General of Posts reported that there were around 100 new postal agencies, all set up by individual companies. The Government has begun the initial stages of research into the expansion of the existing railway network, and is encouraging the private sector to participate and invest in this project. It is also looking into the partial privatisation of Saudi Arabian Airlines. The Ports Authority already has considerable private sector participation – for example, King Fahd Vessel Repair Yards, and sections of Jeddah Islamic Port and King Abdulaziz Port in Dammam are being handled by private companies. And in April 2003 it was announced that the Ministry of Health had employed a private company to promote its pre- and post-natal healthcare education programme, which has been introduced into more than 85 per cent of the country's hospitals.

Privatisation is seen as a key strategic step for the country's major national industries, at once supplying injections of capital and leading to more efficient management practices. The Jeddah Islamic Port (**above** and **right**) was the flagship of the privatisation process that began in the late 1990s.

In 2002, the British Offset Office declared that it had exceeded its target of £1 billion of inward investment into the Kingdom; it was just one of many indications that foreign participation in the private sector had become a key factor in progress in the Kingdom. The Saudi Arabian General Investment Authority (SAGIA), was set up in April 2000 to promote foreign investment and serve the business community as a one-stop-shop and a mediator between investors and the Government. In the same year, SAGIA implemented the Foreign Investment Law, to allow foreign investors to own property, transfer capital and profits, claim full ownership of their projects and enjoy reduced tax rates. The law protects foreign investors from, among other things, confiscation of property without a court order.

In August 2002, SAGIA passed a new amendment strengthening the legal framework, introducing new tax benefits and permitting foreign ownership of land. In the first four years of its operation, SAGIA had approved over 1,200 licenses for foreign projects, worth over US$11 billion. The telecommunications, insurance and railway sectors have already been opened up to foreign firms, and there is also movement in the energy sector. The Supreme Council for Petroleum and Minerals was in negotiations with eight major energy companies

*Although oil revenues have provided income and employment for the growing Saudi population (**left, top** and **bottom**) it has become increasingly clear in recent years that foreign investment will provide the springboard for efficient development of many sectors of industry.*

SABIC corporate headquarters in Jubail on the Gulf coast of Saudi Arabia. Jubail is home to the majority of SABIC's affiliate companies and is the powerhouse of its manufacturing capability in the Kingdom.

Tourism

The opening up of tourism has represented another possibility for diversification. At present, $8 billion leaves the country each year, as three million Saudi Arabians take their holidays – and their money – abroad. The Government's first aim was to develop domestic tourism, then to encourage visitors from other GCC countries and finally tourists from outside the peninsula. To that effect, it established the Supreme Commission for Tourism in early 2000. In July 2001, the foundation stone of the Prince Sultan Tourism and Hotel Management College was laid in Abha.

Saudi Arabian Airlines naturally plays a major part in the tourism drive, and reported a record 13.7 million passengers in 2001. The majority were Muslim pilgrims flying in to perform the Hajj. Over 80 per cent of annual demand for hotel space in Makkah and Madinah occurs over a six-week period surrounding the pilgrimage. The Government is trying to capitalise on the huge numbers of visitors – 2.3 million foreigners and 700,000 Saudis in 2000 – who come to perform the Hajj and the "minor" pilgrimage, the *Umrah*.

Tourist visas are now being issued to visitors, allowing them to travel to parts of the country beyond the two Holy Cities, and to experience the national parks and forests, the beaches and historic sites throughout the country. Forecasts predict three million or more people visiting the country on tourist visas, annually generating around $2.7 billion in revenue. The Government predicts that by 2020 the country would have 50,000 hotel rooms and between 1.5 and 2.3 million Saudis trained in the tourism sector.

The many attractions to interest and entertain tourists include (**clockwise from above**) the new cable cars in the Asir, an exhibition of classic cars at the King Abdul Aziz Foundation for Research and Archives, the carved rockfaces of the Nabatean remains at Medain Saleh, and the mud-brick ruins at Dir'iyyah.

in 2005, including ExxonMobil, Royal Dutch/Shell and BP Amoco, to invest in the Kingdom's energy to the tune, initially at least, of $25 billion. In April 2003, the Minister of Petroleum and Mineral Resources heralded a new mining strategy which would bolster private investment in the mining sector. The new law would allow foreign investors to join Saudi companies in exploring the country's mineral resources, among which phosphate, iron ore, bauxite, zinc, gold and copper are numbered.

Interestingly enough, Saudi Arabia is currently the largest economy outside the World Trade Organisation (WTO). The Government is committed to becoming a member, and to that effect has passed more than 22 trade-related laws since the 1990s, with 19 more in the pipeline. The Kingdom has already signed bilateral trade agreements with 13 countries, and in 2005 was in the process of negotiating with a further 16 trading partners. WTO membership would require Saudi Arabia to commit fully to reform, development, liberalisation, openness and diversification of its economy. By 2005 the signs were that the Government was prepared for this, and is committed to the process. It has pledged to speed up all pending bilateral negotiations, to put in place all the rules and laws required for accession to the WTO, to conclude ongoing negotiations between the Gulf Cooperation Council (GCC) and the European Union on issues related to the Free Trade Area, to support non-petroleum exports, to foster and encourage small and medium-sized enterprises, and to review all existing bureaucratic controls, red tape and taxes in order to smooth procedures and help nurture a healthy and functioning business environment.

A simultaneous development in economic reform was the so-called "Charter to Reform the Arab Stand". That initiative encouraged economic and political reforms, as well as greater economic integration in the region, and broader participation by Arab citizens in the political process. It called on Arab states to form a Greater Arab Free Trade Area (GAFTA), which was to result in unified tariffs and duties by the end of 2005, and the eventual establishment of a Common Arab Market (CAM). All members of the Arab League were being encouraged to modernise their economies, privatise government-owned industries and open up economic development to outside participation.

The Government was swift to announce that it was divesting itself of 20 state assets. This would bring in considerable new revenue, which would in turn help to bring down debt, shore up private sector growth and create more employment opportunities. Talk of monetary union, and eventually perhaps a single currency among GCC countries, were already in play. For Saudi Arabia, membership of such a union would be broadly positive. A new insurance law was under discussion, which would provide a regulatory framework and was bound to attract more foreign direct investment, while the whole area of company law and corporate governance was under review to make it more transparent, and therefore more attractive. A new capital markets law was set to increase transparency and put the country's stock market on a comparable footing with Western bourses in terms of regulations for investment, which would be another huge improvement. Meanwhile, the telecommunications and transport industries looked to be among the most healthy non-oil sectors, and if they continued to grow and flourish, they would offset any decline in oil receipts and put the Saudi economy on a more balanced footing.

Amid all this expansion, the social and religious values of Islam remained the permanent matrix for all ministers, reformers and businesses. For a Muslim, one of the cornerstones of the faith is the requirement to give alms, and this principle is the foundation of Saudi Arabia's welfare state. Free education, medical services, pensions and social insurance have been provided for many years now, and are expanding together with subsidies on agriculture, housing and imported food. The trick in the coming years will be the Government's ability to balance increased growth, openness and diversification with the needs of the poor and unemployed, and, most importantly, to create an economic environment that fosters and supports the true spirit of Saudi enterprise.

Central in Saudi Arabia's economic prospects are oil and gas, of which the country has the world's largest reserves. The hydrocarbons look set to be an essential global commodity long into the future.

The Labour Market

Theoretically, Saudi Arabia's economy generates enough jobs to ensure almost full employment for the country's available workforce. The service sector in particular is a huge employer, providing jobs for almost half the working population and pumping more than US$80 billion into the economy each year. The problem, and the reason that unemployment is now such a pressing concern in the Kingdom, is that of the country's 7.6 million employees, an estimated two-thirds are foreign workers. In the days of the massive infrastructural development of the 1970s, expatriate workers – primarily from other Arab states and from Asia – were brought in to assist in the design and construction of new highways, ports, cities and housing. This influx naturally brought about social stresses, not least the most obvious challenge of where to house the incomers. Over 30 new towns and some 75 new municipalities were created, at huge cost. At the time, it would have been almost impossible to create a productive economy and a modern infrastructure based on a Saudi-only workforce, and these measures were essential. However, even after the main phase of development had ended, foreign workers continued to stream into the country in expectation of a living.

Although approximately 160,000 jobs are being created each year, these new positions are almost equally divided between Saudis and expatriate workers. The unemployment rate has continued to rise – from 8.1 per cent in 1999 to over 9 per cent four years later, and worryingly for the Government, the labour force was continuing to grow at a rate of five per cent per annum. Two-fifths of the indigenous population is now below 15 years of age, and it is no secret that these young people are leaving school with fewer prospects than the generation before them. Estimates suggest that the number of jobseekers could grow to 4.8 million by 2010.

The Government is fully aware of the challenges ahead. As early as 1995 it had already launched the concept of "Saudization", a scheme which aims to increase the participation of Saudis in the workforce in all sectors of the economy. The two pillars of Saudization are the steady reclamation of jobs currently filled by expatriates, and the filling of new positions by trained Saudi workers. The first four years of the scheme were not overly successful, as irregular enforcement resulted in an increase rather than a drop in the number of expatriate workers; and a total of 380,000 Saudis joined the ranks of the unemployed between 1995-1999.

However, things are steadily improving, and a decrease in the number of residence permits being granted to foreigners, particularly Europeans, is already having an effect. One of the main engines driving the increase in employment opportunities is the information technology sector, which is playing a pivotal role in turning around Saudi Arabia's socio-economic outlook. Information technology is seen as one of the core sectors of the new economy, and because it is still in the development stage, jobs and business opportunities abound. However, there is a further complication. The country currently finds itself in the paradoxical position of having an increasing number of jobs to offer to a growing percentage of inexperienced nationals. Saudis are still having to compete with a large number of – often more experienced – expatriate workers.

Training is therefore key, and the development of Saudi human capital has been put to the top of the agenda. Early in the new century the Government founded the Human Resources Development Fund (HRDF), which subsidises the cost of training Saudi workers in private sector companies, and offers wage-sharing schemes to businesses who employ Saudis. Steps have also been taken to improve the enforcement of Saudization. The HRDF programme is still not widespread enough to support all applicants, and there is a constant balance to be achieved between offering adequate jobs for the young, while at the same time defending the competitiveness of local businesses. But the Government is fully aware that the only way for the country's global and highly competitive job market to survive and prosper is to implement a 'recruit, retain and retrain' policy, ensuring that education and learning does not stop when a graduate leaves school or university, but continues throughout his working life, with ongoing training and a constant strengthening of his knowledge and skills base.

The increased participation of women in the labour market, many of them highly educated, has also brought benefits. At present, just over 10 per cent of the female population are employed in hospitals, schools, certain government positions, banking and the retail and leisure sectors, and this is expected to increase. Saudi women are also becoming more active in business, and several business groups have sprung up across the country dedicated specifically to them. Estimates suggest that Saudi women are owners or part-owners of over 22,000 businesses, and thousands of women invest in stocks.

In the coming years, Saudization is to be further fine-tuned, and businesses will be encouraged to lower the number of expatriate workers even further. Training schemes are to be improved and increased – the Government is committed to this policy, and is currently spending 7.5 per cent of GNP on education and training – far higher than many countries including the US and UK. The Saudi Government is serious about meeting the challenge of restructuring the country's job market, and has devised a set of policies that will allow its workforce to survive in an increasingly competitive global arena.

Opposite:

Key in the "Saudization" drive, has been ensuring the workforce is trained to take over from the expatriates they are replacing. This is now taking place and the number of Saudi nationals at work is increasing.

Oil and Gas

The history of oil and its transformation of the Middle East is one of the great stories of the twentieth century. Today, oil and gas revenues provide approximately 90 per cent of Saudi Arabia's total export earnings, 70-80 per cent of state revenues and around 40 per cent of the country's GDP, but the harnessing of Arabia's "black gold" took some time and great patience.

It all began back in the latter years of the nineteenth century, when huge "lakes of oil" were discovered in Iraq in 1871 and in Iran in 1908. Then in the 1920s, an enterprising New Zealander named Major Frank Holmes went to Bahrain and managed to obtain an oil concession there. For want of enough manpower and money to maintain the operation however, his concession on the mainland lapsed, and eventually it was turned over to an oil company based in the United States, a subsidiary of the Standard Oil Company of California (then called SOCAL, today known as Chevron). SOCAL was one of the largest oil producers in the USA, but their overseas explorations had thus far yielded nothing. It was not long before SOCAL's geologists were on their way to Jeddah for an audience with the founder of the modern Saudi state, King Abdul Aziz ibn Abdul Rahman Al Saud. It was he who first opened the door to the development of his country's vast resources. In 1933, he granted a concession to SOCAL, and by the end of that year, eight American oilmen were working in the Dammam area. Five years later, while drilling at Well No 7 in Dhahran, the first oil was discovered, and the destiny of the country would change for ever.

The first tanker was loaded and its cargo exported in 1939. In 1944 the company's name was changed to the Arabian American Oil Company (Aramco), and in 1948 ownership was divided between SOCAL, Mobil, Exxon and Texaco. The discovery and development of Saudi Arabia's many oil fields had begun slowly – the Second World War and its aftermath meant that transportation problems and material shortages were the norm. But with the ending of hostilities, production picked up, and Aramco's crude oil production increased from 20,000 barrels a day before 1944 to 500,000 by the end of 1949. In 1950, a 1,700 kilometre Trans-Arabian pipeline, known as Tapline, was completed. It linked the oil fields of the Eastern Province with Lebanon and the Mediterranean. Throughout these years, new oil fields continued to be discovered and exploited. The Saudi Government began to increase its participation in the exploration and extraction of oil, and in the late 1950s Government ministers began to join Aramco's Board of Directors. In 1962, the Government established the General Petroleum and Mineral Organisation (Petromin), the State's petroleum company. Petromin's role was to maximise the use of the oil, gas and mineral reserves, to engage foreign partners, to exploit natural resources such as the evolution of a wide range of hydrocarbon products like petroleum, LPG (Liquid Petroleum Gas) and asphalt, and to market these products both domestically and internationally. Refining, pipelines, storage, prospecting for precious metals and power generation all fall within Petromin's remit.

Exploration for oil and gas continued through the 1960s, 1970s and 1980s to establish as precisely as possible the extent of the country's reserves. Year by year, more oil was discovered than was pumped. By 1974, Aramco was producing 8.2 million barrels a day. The country's known reserves, almost double any other country's, amount to over one-third of the world's total. By 1985, 59 commercial fields had been discovered, 17 of them offshore, three partially so, and the rest onshore. The Ghawar field is the world's largest field onshore, and Safaniya the largest offshore. The great size of the country's oil resources, the ruggedly hostile nature of the terrain, the distances over which the oil must be transported and the vast infrastructure of men and machines required to extract the oil, call for the most modern technology, much of which has been developed in Saudi Arabia by Aramco.

In 1972, the Saudi Government acquired a 25 per cent interest in Aramco's crude oil concessions rights. In 1974 this was increased to a controlling 60 per cent, and the final takeover was completed in 1980, by which time Saudi oil officials had long been responsible for all aspects of the kingdom's oil policy. The Saudi Arabian Oil Company, known as Saudi Aramco, was set up by Royal Decree in 1988. It is the world's largest oil-producing company, and from its headquarters in Dhahran on the east coast, it controls almost all the Kingdom's vast hydrocarbon enterprises, and engages in all activities related to the oil industry, on a commercial basis.

Saudi Aramco undertakes the exploration of the Kingdom's reserves of crude oil and natural gas, and exploits this natural treasure. It has the capacity to produce up to ten million barrels of crude oil per day on a sustained basis, and currently supplies 11 per cent of the world's oil demand. It manufactures a wide range of petroleum products, and markets oil, gas and petroleum products both domestically and internationally. The company owns five refineries – at Ras Tannurah, Riyadh, Jeddah, Rabigh and Yanbu – and has become a vital part of the entire fabric of Saudi Arabian society. The company is the largest single employer in the country, outside the Government. The wages it pays and the goods and services it buys in the local market help fuel the regional and

The discovery of the reserves of "black gold" came conveniently to Saudi Arabia at a time of need, but the extent of its impact has long surpassed anything the first prospectors can have imagined. Seventeen of the Kingdom's 59 commercial fields operate offshore.

national economy. Saudi Aramco has built over 100 schools in the Eastern Province, has helped develop the Province's electrical power grid and carried out other infrastructure and educational projects, such as its Mobile Library Project, which provides books for children in remote areas, in order to foster a love of reading at a young age. It also provides high quality housing and recreational facilities for its employees, both Saudi nationals and expatriates, who benefit from the provision of medical care, training and other services.

On the environmental front, Saudi Aramco has developed a comprehensive plan for dealing with oil spills, and employs the latest response technology and training methods. It played an important role in containing the 1991 war-generated Gulf oil spill – the world's largest such disaster. Saudi Aramco is consistently ranked top among the major international oil companies by *Petroleum Intelligence Weekly*. Every year, the *Weekly* chooses the largest 50 oil companies, and ranks them based on six criteria: the company's operations; the volume of oil and gas reserves; the volume of production; the capacity of the refineries and the size of the oil production sale. Consistently since 1993, Saudi Aramco has come out top in all six criteria, something of which the entire country is justifiably proud.

Saudi Arabia is, naturally, a key member of the Organisation of Petroleum Exporting Countries (OPEC), and throughout the oil price boom of the 1970s played an important role in stabilising prices, voluntarily acting as OPEC's "swing producer" during the 1970s and 1980s, and cutting its own quota by up to 50 per cent in order to maintain the overall proportion of OPEC production within the limits agreed. The Government has stated that it remains a policy not to abandon the course it pursued in these years, in order to avoid rapid fluctuations in the price of oil. In 1967, Saudi Arabia submitted a proposal to both Kuwait and Libya for establishing an Arab organisation of petroleum exporting countries, a move which resulted in the formation of OAPEC, which has its headquarters in Kuwait.

The Government of Saudi Arabia has long realised that no matter how large its hydrocarbon resources are, they will not last for

ever. Therefore there has been, and still is, a pressing need to maximise the benefits of technology to exploit the by-products of the oil extraction and refining process. The Saudi Arabian Basic Industries Corporation (SABIC) was formed as the Middle East's largest non-oil company, and accounts for ten per cent of the world's petrochemical production. It operates 16 complexes with international firms, producing products such as petrochemicals, plastics and fertilisers. In 2001, SABIC awarded three international companies contracts to build a major new petrochemical complex at Jubail Industrial City.

The former wasteful flaring of the gas produced in association with crude oil has long since been replaced by a massive master gas-gathering system for the oilfields of the Eastern Province. This system, operated by Saudi Aramco, allows the country to utilise almost all of the gas associated with the onshore production of oil. Some of this gas is used for re-injection into the oilfields to maintain the pressure necessary for extracting oil, while an increasing amount is used for the desalination of water. As part of the Kingdom's plan to optimise its gas resources, the Royal Commission for Jubail and Yanbu implemented in the mid-1970s a two-stage project to conserve and exploit natural gas reserves in the Eastern Region. A 730-mile double pipeline now runs from east to west across the country, transporting oil and gas from Jubail on the Arabian Gulf to Yanbu on the Red Sea in order to supply energy for the many industrial projects undertaken at Yanbu, and to facilitate the export of energy products from the Red Sea coast. It provides a strategically vital alternative to the tanker route through the Strait of Hormuz and saves 3,550 miles of sailing around the peninsula for supplies to the petrochemicals industry at Yanbu.

More recently, the Government has begun to open up its oil and gas industry to foreign participation, for the first time since Aramco was nationalised. In 2002, a consortium of international oil companies were invited to participate in a project to explore for gas in the country's remote Empty Quarter, in a bid to guarantee further development in the exploitation of the country's massive gas reserves. Similarly, there are several joint ventures in the petrochemicals sector already up and running between Saudi Aramco and international players such as ExxonMobil, ChevronTexaco, Royal Dutch/Shell, BP and TotalFinaElf.

Such moves are vital in order to fuel long-term economic development, since it is an absolute given that oil will continue to play a key role in the economy of the country. Even the most conservative estimates of the country's reserves stand at over 250,000 million barrels, with proven gas reserves at 5.8 trillion cubic metres. The Kingdom's development plans continue to use oil revenues in order to diversify the Saudi Arabian economy and expand the non-oil industrial sector in order to strengthen the country as a whole. With the much-vaunted electric car still a remote prospect in spite of earlier speculation, oil and gas will remain essential commodities long into the future.

Estimating the extent of hydrocarbon reserves is key to strategic energy planning globally. More pressing in the short term is the actual exploitation of these reserves. As oil prices fluctuate in response to world events, Saudi Arabia has an exceptional capacity to increase or decrease the world's flow, crucial to maintaining a healthy pricing policy for oil internationally.

Outside investors and expertise continue to play a key role in exploiting reserves efficiently. The transfer of these specialist roles to Saudi nationals plays an increasing part in staffing for the oil extraction and refining processes shown here (the refinery at Ras Tannurah, **above**, with settlement tanks, **left**) ensuring that Saudi Arabia can become largely self-sufficient in terms of manpower needs.

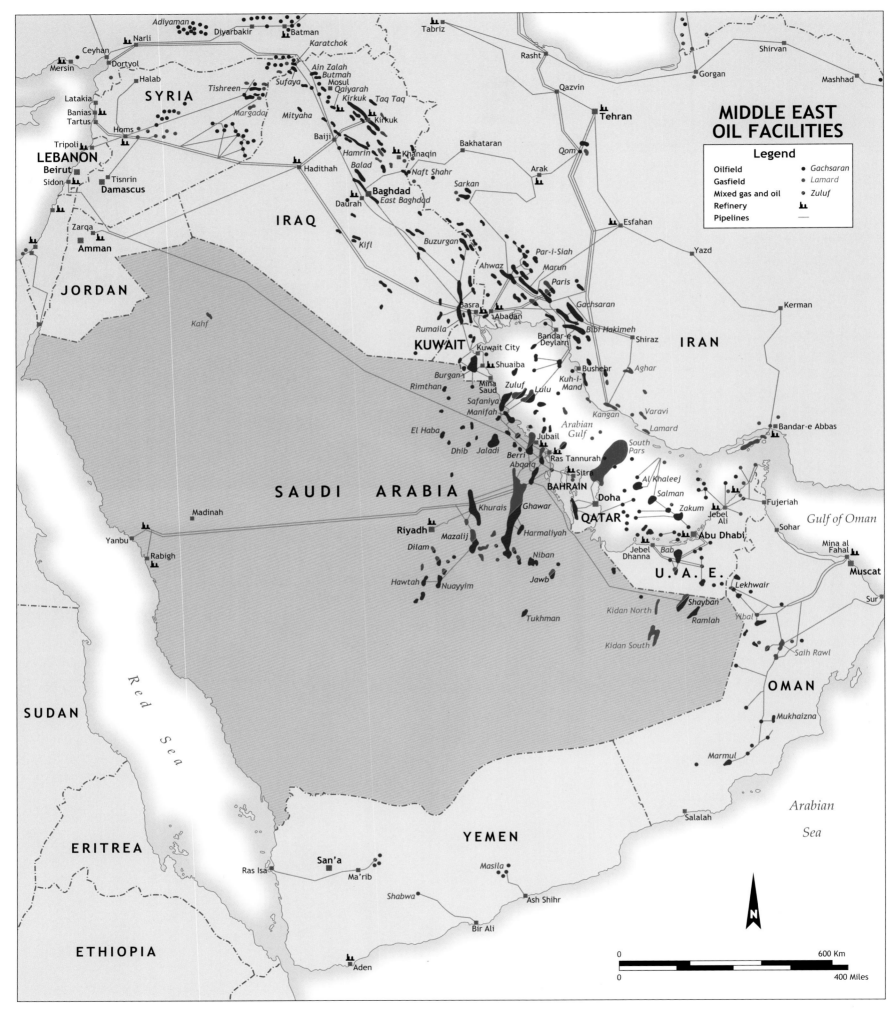

MIDDLE EAST OIL FACILITIES

Legend

Oilfield	● Gachsaran
Gasfield	● Lamard
Mixed gas and oil	● Zuluf
Refinery	
Pipelines	—

Manufacturing

The reliance of Saudi Arabia's economy on a non-renewable asset has led to a determination from within the Government to diversify by building up the non-oil sector. Industry, especially hydrocarbon based, has already become a major source of income, and has, in a relatively short space of time, turned the Kingdom from an importer to an exporter of industrial products, with over 3,000 factories employing more than 300,000 workers, producing goods that are exported to over 100 countries.

The chemicals sector tops the industries' list, followed by the manufacture of plastic materials, ceramics, construction materials, textiles, readymade clothes, mineral products and foodstuffs.

Since the mid-1970s, the Government's semi-autonomous Saudi Industrial Development Fund (SIDF) has provided viable industrial ventures with cheap finance to start up businesses and joint ventures. In 1976, the Saudi Basic Industries Corporation (SABIC) was established by Royal Decree in order to set up and operate hydrocarbon and mineral-based industries and encourage private sector participation in the nation's economic growth. It has so far invested capital of close to $30 billion, and has become the backbone of Saudi Arabia's successful industrialisation drive. SABIC's marketing activities extend to more than 90 countries, through 18 industrial complexes, with a production capacity of more than 25 million tons.

There are no fewer than eight industrial cities in Saudi Arabia, including those for intermediate chemicals, polymers, plastics, industrial gases, fertilisers, steel and other metals. SABIC employs more than 16,000 workers and trainees, over 72 per cent of whom are Saudi nationals.

The industrial cities at Jubail and Yanbu have played a key role in the Kingdom's drive to develop hydrocarbon-based and energy-intensive industries. The Royal Commission for Jubail and Yanbu, established by Royal Decree in 1975, has created the infrastructure for these two cities. Jubail is the largest, with 17 basic industrial plants, 16 secondary industrial plants

and 100 supporting and light industries plants, as well as a dedicated desalination plant, a vocational training institute and a college. Its 70,000 full-time residents enjoy landscaped parks, sports grounds, beaches and a programme of cultural events, in addition to excellent educational and healthcare facilities. Yanbu meanwhile, located 350 kilometres north-west of Jeddah, is another major industrial site, with a key port, King Fahd Industrial Port, which is the largest oil and petrochemical exporting complex on the Red Sea, and handles the crude oil from the Eastern Province that is delivered through the East-West Pipeline. By the year 2000, Yanbu had over 70,000 full-time residents, and over 50 plants. The Yanbu Petrochemicals Company (YANPET), a joint venture with Mobil, went into production in 2001. It produces ethylene, polyethylene and ethylene glycol, and is one of the largest and most efficient petrochemicals producers in the world, with a total capacity of 1.7 million tonnes per year.

The country has also developed a healthy fertiliser industry. Three world class fertiliser companies, all under the aegis of SABIC, produce a total of 5.5 million metric tons of fertiliser per year, using the most advanced production technology available.

The Government is fully aware that it needs to build on the achievements since the 1970s in order to continue the country's successful economic growth and diversification. The Seventh Development Plan (2000-04) was predicated upon an average annual growth rate of eight per cent for the non-oil industry. A major part of the strategy is the opening up of the economy to privatisation as a strategic option to boost efficiency and productivity.

*Within a space of two or three decades Saudi Arabia's manufacturing sector has become a major source of the nation's income. The production of cement (**right**), styrene (**below**), synthetic lubricants (**opposite, below**) and fertiliser (**opposite, above**) all drive the economy forward.*

Agriculture

The story of Saudi Arabia's agricultural development is extraordinary. In the early 1970s, this vast country, which at 1.45 million square kilometres represents over 1.5 per cent of the world's land mass, was in great part a parched and barren desertscape, relieved only by a few dusty shrubs. Any agriculture that there was amounted to little more than a few small plots of wheat or tomatoes, carefully tended by groups of subsistence farmers. Even by the end of the 1970s, with the introduction of co-operatives, more rural roads and higher investment levels, the agricultural sector was looking slow and unprofitable, as farmers flocked to the new wealth of the cities, creating labour shortages on the farms and in the fields. At the start of the 1980s, the Government announced its four goals for agriculture: to achieve self-sufficiency in basic foodstuffs, to ensure a constant supply of clean water, to balance rural development and employment with that in the cities and to encourage the growth of the private sector in farming and food processing. It must have seemed to many like a distinctly over-ambitious dream. Yet twenty years on, Saudi Arabia's agricultural sector was one of the Kingdom's great success stories. Through the twin lures of heavy subsidies to farmers and investment in public infrastructure, all four goals were realised, and the country stands today as the most efficient agricultural producer in the Middle East.

There are still vast expanses of parched desert, but thanks to a system of pivot-based irrigation these are now relieved by farms, grazing land and huge circular wheat fields, some a kilometre in diameter, which yield great quantities of high-quality grain. Wheat production reached a peak in 1992, with over four million tonnes produced, but by 1999, production had been reduced to a more sustainable level of two million tonnes, where it stands today, making the country the largest wheat producer in the Middle East.

The lack of arable land means that the country still has to import the majority of its food needs, but the Government's programme of improved roads and water resources, combined with research and training centres,

Opposite and below:
Pivot-based irrigation systems have ensured that Saudi Arabia's agricultural development, even in the most parched of regions, has a strong yield. It is the largest producer of wheat in the Middle East.

*Irrigation, as in Hofuf, (**left**), is key in hot climate agricultural practice, as is the re-use of water. With no rivers and diminishing ground reserves, the number of desalination plants like that at al-Jubail, (**right**), looks set to increase.*

agricultural colleges and interest-free loans through the Saudi Arabian Agricultural Bank, has meant that the country exports not only wheat but also dairy produce, poultry, fish, fruit and vegetables to over 45 countries. The Kingdom is self sufficient in egg production, and produces around 140,000 tons of eggs per year. Dairy products have been another success story - in 2000, the Al Safi Dairy at Al-Kharj entered *The Guinness Book of Records* as the largest integrated dairy farm in the world. Saudi Arabia is also the world's largest date producer, with around 400 different varieties and 30 factories handling an annual production of over 35,000 tons of dates and date products, while in the waters of the Red Sea and Arabian Gulf, Saudi fishermen are hauling an annual catch of over 54,000 tons. Watermelons and tomatoes, onions, grapes and citrus fruit are all being exported, and at Jizan, in the Kingdom's verdant south-western corner, farmers have begun to produce tropical fruits like pineapples, bananas, mangoes and guavas.

The Kingdom's agricultural progress was from the start a cause close to King Fahd's heart. In 1997, in recognition of the country's role in agricultural development, the achievement of food security and its contribution to combating hunger, he was awarded the International Agricultural Gold Medal by the Food and Agricultural Organisation.

Water

Saudi Arabia's agricultural success story would have been impossible without irrigation. The country may be blessed with the world's largest oil reserves, but it remains thirsty for a liquid more precious still – fresh water. Saudi Arabia is the largest country in the world without rivers, and rainfall rarely exceeds a meagre 100 mm per year. Steep population growth rates, a new wave of industrial projects in areas such as Jubail and Yanbu, together with very high usage in the agriculture sector – which accounts for more than 85 per cent of the total annual water consumption – means that water resources are becoming scarcer. Groundwater is a diminishing resource, and although underground water is thought to equal the annual flow of the Nile for 600 years, that too is finite. The building of dams and desalination plants has been a key policy since the 1980s, with 206 dams in operation and another 11 under construction, plus 30 desalination plants which provide 50 per cent of the country's water requirements and supply the cities of Jeddah, Makkah, Madinah and Taif among others. However, a number of these plants are beyond their half-life, and will be decommissioned in less than 15 years, while at the same time, water requirements are projected

to increase to 7.1 million cubic metres a day by 2020, up from the present level of 4.5 million cubic metres per day.

In the summer of 2002 therefore, the Water Affairs Ministry embarked on a programme aimed at quenching the country's thirst. By drafting a national water plan, the Ministry brought all the separate issues – domestic consumption, agriculture and industry – under one umbrella, and put in place a comprehensive system to guarantee that the Kingdom would not run dry. The first step, says the Deputy Minister, is to evaluate all the existing water resources in the kingdom, and to maximise the efficiency of its collection. The next step is to try and balance the provision of affordable water for every household, with the freeing up of more funds so that the government can invest in other aspects of the water sector. At the moment, although water used for domestic consumption is not free of charge, the cost is remarkably low. By 2005, the subsidised rate was to be replaced by a new tariff structure, plus a country-wide metering system, aimed at measuring consumption and increasing cost recovery not only for domestic usage but also on the agricultural and industrial side.

The agricultural sector was to come under particular scrutiny. At the time of writing, water is distributed free of charge, but in future, farmers would be subject to meters and tariffs. The Ministry also wants to maximise efficiency in agriculture, and increase productivity per unit of water used. Farmers will be encouraged to use new irrigation techniques and to look into growing crops that use less water. Another part of the strategy is to raise awareness among the population of the importance of conserving, rather than wasting, water. Part of the reason for the country's high consumption levels – Saudi Arabia's per capita domestic water consumption stands at around 230 litres per day, compared to France's 150 litres per day – is to do with lifestyle.

Many people live in big houses, with gardens, fountains and pools. Ample flowing water, in a country surrounded by desert, is seen as a luxury and a status symbol. The Government will encourage householders to install domestic appliances such as washing machines and lavatory flushers that use less water.

The total cost of building, operating and maintaining water projects to guarantee a 200 litre per day consumption level is estimated at $34 billion. The Government is encouraging the private sector to become much more involved, and in 2002, structural changes in the government resulted in the creation of a unified electricity and water ministry, a logical combination given Saudi Arabia's dependence on desalination plants, which use large amounts of electricity.

Plans are under way for the construction of four large independent water and power plants under the aegis of the Saudi Electricity Company and the Saline Water Conversion Corporation, with the involvement of private investors. HSBC Investment Bank, the German engineering firm Fichtner, a legal team from Clifford Chance and the law firm of Yousef and Mohammed Al-Jadaan were selected in early 2003 to advise on the programme.

One thing is certain. While countries such as Kuwait are already looking into importing fresh water from neighbouring countries, Saudi Arabia will not go down that road. Such an option exposes any country to a high risk of political instability, and the Government is committed to remaining self-sufficient in its water supply at all costs.

Mining

As well as oil and gas, Saudi Arabia is also blessed with considerable mineral resources, including gold and silver, steel industry metals and a wide range of industrial metals. The country's underground wealth has long been exploited. Three thousand years ago, a mine some 180 miles north of Jeddah known as Mahad al-Dhahab (Cradle of Gold) was a rich source of gold, copper and silver for the inhabitants of that region. By the 1990s, gold had been discovered at 600 sites around the Kingdom. The Mahad al-Dhahab mine was re-opened by Petromin, with the intention of developing a high-grade underground gold mine with a capacity of 400 tons of ore per day. Silver and base metal deposits, including bauxite, copper, iron, lead, tin and zinc, as well as non-metallic minerals such as bentonite, diatomite, fluorite, potash and high-purity silica sand have all been discovered, indicating the range of further treasure buried deep beneath the Kingdom's soil.

In 1997, the Saudi Arabian Mining Company (Ma'aden) was created as a catalyst for private sector investment. It produces quantities of gold, silver, copper and zinc from a range of mines around Dhahab, Asir and on the eastern margin of the Arabian Shield, 250 kilometres west of Riyadh. The largest single project occupying the Ma'aden planners at present is the deposit of phosphates at Al Jalamid in the north of the Kingdom. They have been negotiating with an international consortium to develop the phosphate resources there. Phosphate is a significant source of fertiliser, and proven resources at Al-Jalamid are sufficient to mine 4.5 million tons of phosphate rock per year for over half a century.

In 1999, the Saudi Geological Survey was established as an independent organisation to conduct all geological survey operations for the Kingdom's onshore and offshore areas.

Left:
Water for industrial cooling circulates through a 25-km-long system near al-Jubail, pumped out of the sea at a rate equal to two-thirds of the combined flow of the Tigris and the Euphrates.

Opposite:
Saudi Arabia has the largest mineral deposits in the Gulf, and the Saudi Geological Survey has done extensive work to catalogue over one thousand sites of precious metals. The Ministry of Petroleum and Mineral Resources is keen to encourage further foreign investment in this sector.

Electricity

Saudi Arabia's electricity sector has been constantly expanding for half a century. In a country where summer temperatures regularly reach 45°C, a reliable source of electricity to power air conditioning, freezers and refrigerators is vital. In the early days of the country's development, the generation of electricity was left to small local companies in towns and villages throughout the country, selling the power they produced at varying rates according to the local cost of electricity generation. In 1961, the Department of Electricity Affairs was established to govern all these individual activities. The General Electricity Corporation was set up, representing the Government's equity holdings in these electricity generating companies and with overall responsibility for the Kingdom's electricity system. Then in 1998 it was announced that the Kingdom's ten electricity companies would be consolidated into a single stock market company, the Saudi Electrical Company (SEC). In February 2000 the ten separate companies signed a merger agreement. The Government eventually aims to sell its 85 per cent holding in SEC and bring in private investors.

Meanwhile, electricity demand is growing at 4.5 per cent or more each year on year. Demand outstripped supply long ago, due to a growing population and electricity subsidies which encourage over-usage and waste. As early as 1995, the Government took steps to improve efficiency, by raising rates for electricity for both businesses and private consumers in a bid to curb demand and encourage conservation. The authorities also plan to increase installed power generation capacity from 20,000 mw at the end of the 1990s to 69,000 mw by 2020.

Some companies, such as the Saudi Arabian Oil Company (Saudi Aramco), have started to make their own electricity provision in order to lessen dependence on the regional power grid. Electricity generation is a natural candidate for further privatisation. The first private-sector enterprise will come with a proposed new plant being built on a build-operate-transfer basis for the Saudi Petrochemical Company (Sadaf) in Jubail. The winning contractor will operate the plant for a period of 20 months before transferring it to Sadaf.

*Saudi Arabia now has one comprehensive national electricity grid, feeding all major cities such as Jeddah, pictured (**below**), in some areas carrying power across vast tracks of desert to reach areas of demand (**left**).*

Infrastructure

In terms of amenities and communications, the Kingdom was transformed in the 1970s with a massive programme of construction and infrastructure development, all fuelled by oil wealth. Contractors came from around the world to take part in the dizzying task of building a modern nation almost from scratch. Although the furious pace of construction had slowed down considerably by the mid-1980s, new infrastructure projects continued to flow, and the urban and rural landscape kept evolving, as it is still doing to this day.

The road network of Saudi Arabia was transformed during the 1970s when the length of paved roads tripled and the rural network grew fivefold. With the massive increase in traffic that has come about thanks to the development of the agriculture sector in rural areas, and the exponential growth in the number of car owners in the cities, more and more roads are constantly being built. Dozens of flyovers, eight-lane motorways, ring roads, underpasses and overpasses all help ease traffic flow.

Saudi Arabia is linked by road to Jordan, Yemen, Kuwait, Qatar and the UAE, but probably the most impressive road construction project of all has been the construction of the King Fahd Causeway, connecting the Saudi Arabian mainland with the island of Bahrain. The cornerstone of this four-lane highway was laid in 1982, and the 26 kilometres of road was completed in 1986. It is used by about 3.6 million passengers per year, coming and going.

Saudi Arabia's railway network is the only rail system in the Arabian peninsula. Because of the vast distances involved, often in extreme environmental conditions such as desert sand and fierce temperatures, the rail network is not nearly as developed as the roads and airport infrastructure. At present the network consists of a 571 kilometre single-track line between Riyadh and Dammam, and a 322 kilometre line between Riyadh and Hufuf.

The Government has, however, opened the way for the part-privatisation of the railway network, and is encouraging individual companies to invest and participate in the construction of a 950 kilometre line from Riyadh to Jeddah, a 570 kilometre line from Jeddah to Madinah via Makkah, and a 115 kilometre line linking Dammam with Jubail. There is also talk of a northern line from Riyadh to the Jordanian border.

Saudi Arabian Airlines – Saudia – is the national airline, the largest in the Middle East, carrying 12 million passengers each year, mainly on domestic routes. In 2001 it announced a 1.7 per cent increase in passenger numbers, which was remarkable given the events of September 11 that year. Restructuring is in place to prepare Saudia for eventual privatisation.

A private sector airline, National Air Service, was established in 1998 with an initial capitalisation of $320 million, and will undoubtedly develop the air transport sector further.

Jeddah's King Abdul Aziz International airport is larger than Kennedy, Newark and O'Hare combined. A US$1.5 billion expansion programme to enable the airport to handle the world's largest aircraft, including the Super-Jumbo A380 Airbus, was announced in 2005. The airport is expected to accommodate 15 million passengers, many of them Hajj pilgrims, by the year 2010. The newest airport is the King Fahd International airport at Dhahran in the Eastern Province, with the potential to serve 12 million passengers per year.

The busiest of all the Kingdom's ports is the Jeddah Islamic Port, the main port of entry for pilgrims on their way to the Hajj, and the principal commercial port of the country.

Other ports include King Abdul Aziz Port at Dammam, the Commercial Port at Jizan, the Jubail Commercial Port, and the Commercial Port at Yanbu. The latest port is at Dhiba, strategically located at the northern end of the Red Sea coast of Saudi Arabia. It is a natural harbour, sheltered on three sides by hills, and with a spacious hinterland for potential development. Strategically it is extremely important, being the closest port to the Suez Canal.

Above:

The King Fahd Causeway, completed in 1986, provides a vibrant link – societal no less than physical – with the island of Bahrain.

Left:

In the other direction from Dammam, the Canadian-built railway – currently the Kingdom's only railway line – provides a comfortable three hour journey to Riyadh.

Opposite:

*Pending implementation of the plans to construct a vast national railway network, the road provides the Kingdom's primary mode of transport. An immense network of asphalt road (some 30,000 km by the end of the last millennium) crisscrosses the country. Seen here is one of the major interchanges outside Riyadh (**top**) and the ubiquitous Mercedes truck (**bottom**) a familiar sight across the country.*

Telecoms and Technology

In the years since the first telephone exchange was installed in al-Dira in 1930, Saudi Arabia's telecommunications industry has undergone a series of rapid changes, as the pace of development quickened throughout the century. Some of the most dramatic changes came about in the 1990s when the Global System for Mobiles (GSM) was launched in 1996. In that year, just ten per cent of the population (around 1.7 million homes) had land lines, while mobile phones were owned by just 1.1 per cent, or about 200,000 Saudis. By 2003, there were close to five million land lines, and over three million mobile phone subscribers, with the number increasing by 130,000 monthly.

Then came the internet. An internet service was launched in Saudi Arabia 1999, with all connections routed through a state server located at the King Abdul-Aziz City for Science and Technology. This single server meant that costs for users could be high – certainly higher than the international average. In July 2001 therefore, Saudi Telecom launched the ADSL (Assymetric Digital Subscriber Line) service, a broader band width which has reduced the cost of the internet. By 2003 there were 21 Internet Service Providers (ISPs) in the country, providing access to over two million users. All the forecasts have predicted that, given the high number of young people per family home in Saudi Arabia, and the general increase in familiarity with the internet, this figure will have at least doubled within the decade to 2010.

For businesses operating within the country, two crucial questions are the speed and efficiency of the Saudi Internet, and the affordability of its service. The recent introduction of wider internet band width has put the country ahead of neighbouring Kuwait, and has gone some way to addressing these issues.

Following on from the launch of the internet, the next big event in the telecoms arena was the announcement of an Initial Public Offering (IPO) of a 30 per cent stake in the Saudi Telecommunications Company (STC). Sixty million shares at a cost of $44.3

King Abdul Aziz was quick to appreciate how vital a role the telephone would play in bridging the vast distances in his fledgling state. Traditionalists, mistrustful of the alien technology and fearing a threat to traditional social values, were firmly quashed by the new king. The Aramco compound, ever a model township, enjoyed the benefits of the new network early (**above**, an image of installation in 1953). Other communication technologies received a similar mixed reception – wariness versus a burning desire to learn about the world beyond. Satellite television (reception dish shown **left**) was for a period banned. The internet, when it first arrived, was screened to prevent an influx of amoral material. In spite of this, however, it has proved hugely popular. Surfers at al-Samm, one of Riyadh's popular internet cafés are shown **opposite**.

each, went on sale in December 2002. The offer was massively oversubscribed and generated $4 billion, making it the second-largest IPO in the world. It attracted a great deal of interest among ordinary Saudi Arabians, partly because of the sheer novelty value of privatisation - this offer is the first step in a widespread programme of privatisation that the Government has begun to implement. But the interest was mainly due to the profitability of STC itself, and the rapid increase in the price of the shares in the first few months of trading.

The Saudi Telecommunications Company was turned into a corporation in 1998, and issued its first set of accounts in the spring of 2002. These showed that the company had net earnings averaging more than US$1 billion per year. Earnings are continuing to rise, driven by the increase in mobile phone subscribers, and by increased efficiency. In 2001, the company announced that it was separating its core services - fixed lines, mobile services, data communications and the internet - into separate business units, which have the potential eventually to be spun off into autonomous businesses. However, the company was soon to be exposed to outside competition; a second GSM license was to be issued by the end of 2004, and fixed telephone lines were to be opened up to competitors by 2008. The Finnish company Nokia and Sweden's Ericsson have already begun implementing projects to extend the Kingdom's fifth mobile expansion project, which will add three million mobile lines to the present network, which covers more than 100 cities, towns and major highways.

Today, Saudi Arabia is the fifth-largest user of telecommunications facilities in the world. In 1985 it joined the other Arab League nations in launching Arabsat, the Arab world's first communications satellite. Its two primary tracking and control stations are at Riyadh, with further stations at King Fahd Telecommunications City near Jeddah and at Ta'if. The second generation satellite was launched in 1996, and was projected to last until 2012, while the first satellite of the third generation was successfully launched in 1999, and covers the countries of the Middle East, Northern, Central and East Africa, and most of Europe.

7

Society Today

Young Saudi Arabians are growing fast in numbers and are increasingly better educated than the older generation. The internet has brought a much greater awareness of the world beyond the country's borders. The pressure in society to change and to adapt inherited norms and attitudes is considerable. A measure of secularisation is one consequence. Yet the role of the mosque and of Qur'anic disciplines remains central, and is a major factor of stability.

The opening of street cafés is one example of a more relaxed attitude to the communal use of leisure hours.

Government and Constitution

The system of Government in the Kingdom is monarchical. Dynastic right is confined to the sons of Abdul Aziz ibn Saud and their sons. The most eligible of them are invited through the consultative process of *bai'ah* (the confirmation of recognition by the religious scholars, or *ulema*) to rule in accordance with the Holy Quran and the Prophet's Sunnah. The King names and may remove from office the Crown Prince who himself assumes the role of King on the death of the incumbent, pending the outcome of *bai'ah*. The constitution is the Holy Qur'an and the Prophet's Sunnah from which the regime derives its power and which rules over all state laws. The system of government is founded on justice, *shura* ("consultation") and equality in compliance with Islamic *shari'ah* (the revealed law of Islam). The Basic Law is the written set of principles on which the Kingdom operates. It is altered and amended to suit changing circumstances, for example the formation of the Majlis as-Shura and the restructuring of regional government (*see below*). The citizens pledge allegiance to the King on the basis of the Holy Qur'an and Prophet's *sunnah* (the "way" the Prophet lived), as well as on the principle of "hearing is obeying" in both prosperity and adversity.

The Monarchy

The reigning Monarch heads the Government of the Kingdom as Prime Minister. The present King, Adullah bin Abdul Aziz, is known by his title of King and also as the Custodian of the Two Holy Places, to emphasise his role as protector of the holiest places in Islam and the pilgrims who visit them. He is also Commander of the National Guard.

Council of Ministers

The King presides over a cabinet, known as the Council of Ministers, consisting of 28 Ministers. Under him is the First Deputy Prime Minister, the Crown Prince, Prince Sultan bin Abdul Aziz. The other Ministers who serve on the Council are the Ministers of Agriculture, Civil Service, Commerce & Industry, Communications & Information, Defence and Aviation, Economy & Planning, Education, Finance, Foreign Affairs, the Hajj, Health, Higher Education, the Interior, Islamic Affairs, Justice, Labour & Social Affairs, Municipal & Rural Affairs, Petroleum & Mineral Resources, Transport, Water & Electricity and, since the late 1990s, the Secretary-General of the Supreme Commission for Tourism, who holds the rank of Minister. In addition to these Ministers are five other Ministers of State.

The Council was first established in 1953 by King Abdul Aziz. A by-law of 1993 gave it the responsibility of drafting and overseeing the implementation of internal and external financial, economic, educational and defence policies and the general affairs of state. It meets weekly. The Council holds executive power and has the final say in the financial and administrative matters of all the ministries and other government bodies. It also has the responsibility of looking into resolutions passed by the Majlis as-Shura, the Consultative Council.

Majlis as-Shura

The Majlis as-Shura was established by King Fahd in 1993 and marked a significant move towards formalising a more participatory form of government. The primary function of the Majlis is to provide the King with advice on issues of importance. Its members are appointed by the King for a four-year renewable term and represent the broad spectrum of Saudi society. At first the Council consisted of 60 members in addition to the Chairman, but in 2001 the King increased its membership to 120, plus the Chairman. Although the four-year term of service is renewable, this is on the basis that at the end of any term at least half of those appointed to the following session must be new members. Members are chosen to reflect the different aspects of society, and include tribal and religious leaders, business and professional men and government officials. Academics form the largest group. The members are able to initiate legislation and review the domestic and foreign policies of the government and if they do not approve of any government action, such views will have to be referred back to the King, who remains the final arbiter of state affairs. The King also has the power to appoint and dismiss Ministers and Council members and to dissolve the Council, restructure it or appoint a new one at any time. The Council debates and considers a broad range of issues, within an Islamic framework. Its power is, therefore, subordinate to that of King and cabinet, yet the Majlis is a voice through which people's views can be heard.

Regional Government

The Royal Decree which structured the regions listed 13 regions and the cities in which the headquarters of each was to be located: Riyadh Region (Riyadh); Makkah Region (Makkah); Madinah Region (Madinah); Qasim Region (Buraidah); Eastern Region (Dammam); Asir Region (Abha); Tabuk Region (Tabuk); Ha'il Region (Ha'il); Northern Border Region (Arar); Jizan Region (Jizan); Najran Region (Najran); Baha Region (Baha) and al-Jawf Region (Sakakah). Each of the regions has a Governor with the rank of Minister who is himself responsible to the Minister of the Interior. The Governor and his staff have to implement governmental laws and regulations and are responsible for the maintenance of public security and the guaranteeing of individual rights and freedoms within the framework of the Shari'ah law. This is encompassed in the "Law of the Regions".

February 10, 2005, was a significant date in modern Saudi Arabia's history: the first municipal elections, seen by many international commentators as possibly the first step towards a fully representative system of government. Some 1,800 candidates contested 128 seats in and around Riyadh, canvassing vigorously amongst the local communities.

Above:

The Administration Centre for the industrial city of Jubayl with its efficient offices grouped around a refreshing, landscaped court in the middle of the building.

Judicial System

The Saudi judicial system is now unified but before this was achieved the four schools of Islamic law used to govern the courts and the judges' decisions: the Hanbali, Shafii, Hanafi and Maliki schools. Each region followed a different school. The Courts now issue their rulings on the basis of the Holy Qur'an and *Sunnah* and are guided not solely by the opinion of one of the Islamic schools of law. So the judicial system is that of *shari'ah*, or the revealed law of Islam. The Qur'an covers much that is relevant to any age in that it expresses God's commands and prohibitions, but where it does not have a position on a particular aspect of modern life, a Royal Decree will fill this need.

By Royal Decree a hierarchy of courts – Summary Courts, *Shari'ah* Courts and a Commission of Judicial Supervision – have been set up. The Summary Courts are of two types: one of which deals with Bedouin affairs and the other with minor criminal and financial cases in urban areas. The *Shari'ah* or

High Courts consist of three or four judges and try the more serious criminal and financial cases, together with matters of personal status or family law. There is a body, the General Presidency of Scientific Research and Ifta, which issues judicial opinions (*fatwa*) on *shari'ah* matters and conducts Islamic research. Another body, the General Presidency for the Morality Committees, is responsible for maintaining behaviour which is consistent with Islamic teachings. The Mutawwa, or religious police, are the enforcers of this policy, as members of the organisation for the Protection of Virtue and Prevention of Vice, but they do not have power of arrest unless accompanied by a policeman.

The ultimate responsibility for promulgating and implementing legislation remains with the Council of Ministers and with the King himself whose decrees have the force of law. The *ulema*, or religious leaders, have an important part to play in Saudi society, in implementing *shari'ah* law and overseeing religious education and all the mosques in the Kingdom.

The History of The Royal Saudi Air Force

The Royal Saudi Air Force (RSAF) is among the most formidable in the Middle East. AWACS early warning systems give an umbrella of protection. An American deal provided the RSAF with semi-automated capability for centralised surveillance. The Air Force has about 80 F-5s and 167 F-15s. It intends eventually to replace the older F-5s with a smaller number of more up-to-date F-15s. A deal was signed with Britain in 1985 whereby weaponry, including military aircraft and training, were exchanged for oil. Under this project, known as the Yamamah Offset Programme, the Royal Saudi Air Force procured Tornado combat jets (it now has about 120) and light bombers as well as Hawk fighters (about 90 at present), PC-9 aircraft and Maverick air-to-ground missiles. Most of these procurements were made in the 1980s and early 1990s. In recent years Yamamah has concentrated more on sustaining existing aircraft and training pilots and other personnel to maintain and fly them, than on acquiring new aircraft. The Yamamah project employs some 5,000 personnel on maintenance, part of an ongoing commitment. Other missile systems include Hawk, Crotal, Shahin and SAM missiles.

Above: Emir Faisal, later His Majesty King Faisal, was a key figure in the development of the RSAF.

Below: Students of the Technical Studies Institute at graduation parade. From here, they are qualified to enter the RSAF.

Above: A Wapiti at Jeddah in 1930 – one of the first aircraft in the Kingdom. The Governor of Jeddah is seated centre.
Below: A Lightning F-53 takes off. These aircraft, flown by Saudi nationals were highly effective in the conflict with Yemen in 1968.

Above:

The pilot of an RSAF F-5, engaged in the protection of the country's borders, signals a greeting from the cockpit.

Defence

Under the leadership of HRH Prince Sultan ibn Abdul Aziz, the Minister of Defence and Aviation, Saudi Arabia has made a sustained endeavour to build up a sizeable army, air force and navy, all equipped with the latest in modern hardware. To avoid creating an overdependence on any single supplier purchases were made from several Western powers and from China (which, in 1989, sold the Saudi Government surface-to-surface missiles). The defence budget accounts for about 13 per cent of GDP. The total strength of the field forces is about 100,000, of which the Royal Saudi Air Force (RSAF) accounts for 18,000, the Army for 70,000 and the Navy for 12,000.

There are two armies in Saudi Arabia, the regular army and the National Guard. Of different composition and historical background, they are both called upon in times of national emergency. The regular army, slightly bigger than the National Guard, consists of armoured brigades, mechanised brigades, an airborne brigade, a Royal Guard,

and artillery battalions. Its strength is concentrated in a number of large Military Cities strategically chosen to protect the Kingdom's borders and oil installations. Training is carried out in four giant Military Colleges and in the Military Cities. Here soldiers are given a rounded education to fit them for their combat duties as well as service to the community: the armed forces pride themselves on the various civil defence tasks which they undertake in rural areas, in agriculture, construction, teaching, fire-fighting, emergency aid and medical assistance. The army has hospitals in Riyadh and Jeddah caring for the health needs mainly of its personnel and their families.

The National Guard was formed from the descendants of those who fought with King Abdul Aziz, the Ikhwan, and is partly made up of tribal battalions under the command of local sheikhs. It consists of an active fighting force and a reserve. The head of the National Guard since 1962 has been King Abdullah, for most of the period in his former roles of a senior prince and of Crown Prince, and the Guard are intensely loyal to him. It was trained by American and

The Educational Explosion

The number of students passing through the educational system has increased sixfold since the 1970s, with the number of full-time teachers increasing ninefold. This has resulted in a ratio of 15 students to each teacher, one of the lowest ratios on the world. An increasing emphasis has been placed on the study of science and technology, part of an ambitious schools project initiated by the then Crown Prince Abdullah. Seen here are students on a school trip to the Aramco Exhibition at Dhahran viewing an astrolabe (**top left** and **opposite**), petroleum-related vehicles (**centre left**) and a cross section of stratified rock (**left**).

British advisers, who, in the early 1990s converted it to a light mechanised force. It can now move swiftly over the desert with its state-of-the-art firepower and desert vehicles. Huge cantonments have been built to house the Guard and its families and several great hospitals to serve their health needs (*see also* Health).

The Royal Saudi Navy has over the years been transformed from a token force of patrol boats into two modern fleets which include missile boats, frigates, minesweepers, torpedo boats and supply ships, as well as command and communications equipment covering the entire Gulf and Red Sea coastlines of the Kingdom. Saudi Arabia's commitment to the development of a mutual defence structure with the other GCC states was tried and tested during the invasion of Kuwait by Iraq in 1991, when it played a crucial role by air, land and sea, in the rapid resolution of this conflict.

Education

The Prophet Muhammad is reported to have said, "To seek knowledge is obligatory on every Muslim, male or female." Saudi Arabia's birth rate has grown and is still increasing at one of the fastest rates in the world. It has been necessary for the Government to put increasingly large amounts of money into the education sector to fulfill the Prophet's obligation. Education is free. Since the 1960s when there was still a high level of illiteracy in the country, the number of schools and students has grown at a rapid pace, especially in the secondary sector.

Today there are over five million students in 60,000 educational establishments across the Kingdom, a remarkable figure considering that the first Government school was opened only in 1903. The aim of the Seventh Development Plan is to eliminate illiteracy and provide educational opportunities to all citizens of school age, both boys and girls. In the early days of the Kingdom teachers and curricula were imported from abroad: the aim today is to train Saudis to replace the foreign labour force. Male and female education has been consolidated under one Ministry. The emphasis of education is to prepare young people to fill the demands of their

society and to keep abreast of scientific and technological advances. In order to achieve this, curricula and teaching methods are to be reviewed. The problem at present in the Saudi school system is that many pupils drop out or else stay beyond the allotted 12 years of schooling. merely repeating course years The failings have been attributed in part to teacher performance. The Government was pledged in the the first decade of the new century to improve teacher training and to review curricula to ensure that they conform with development needs. Another problem to emerge was the inadequacy of school buildings, most of which are still leased. More were to be built.

Pre-School

The provision of infant education is still limited and the Government wants to intensify public awareness of the need to encourage programmes for pre-school children and to urge the private sector to build more nurseries.

Primary level

Schooling at this level now starts at age six and lasts for six years, at the end of which pupils take the Primary Certificate before entering the intermediate stage. There is a mixed gender intake. In 1999 there were 371,000 children in primary education, roughly half of them girls. This number was calculated at 445,000 in 2005.

Intermediary

A three-year course prepares students either to continue to secondary level and the Baccalaureat, or to vocational school to prepare for a technical education. In the Intermediate schools, projections indicated that the 1999 figure of 321,000 entrants (about half of which were female) had risen to 361,000 (of which, again, half would be female) by 2004.

Secondary level

The secondary stage lasts three years and is followed by the Saudi Baccalaureat (the *tawjihiyyah*) which is the key to the tertiary stage. After one year at secondary school there is a choice of streams, scientific (*ilmi*) or literary (*adabi*). Progression is strictly determined by the end of year exams in May-June, with re-sits in September-October. Numbers of entrants had risen from 230,000 in 1999 to an estimated 277,000 by 2004. More females than males were calculated to be entering secondary education by 2004 (146,000 girls as against 131,000 boys) and to graduate (159,000 girls, 107,000 boys).

Higher Education

In a country where primary education began only in the late 1930s, and where a serious secondary educational programme was only conceived in 1953, it is natural that higher

*King Saud University's atrium (**above**) with cool fountains (**left**) leads into the system of arched corridors (**overleaf**) to take students to the various faculties – a breathtaking setting for the tertiary level education of some of Saudi Arabia's brightest young minds. The university was opened in Riyadh in 1957 and has grown at a dramatic rate, now accommodating 24,000 students, many of them girls.*

education was at first given a lower priority than general education. But once the programme of general education had been established in the early 1970s, King Faisal himself directed that special attention should be given to the post-school level.

The Government now provides tertiary education through universities, girls' colleges, military colleges and some other Government agencies. Under the last Development Plan, the Sixth, an exceptional figure, SR 35 billion, was allocated to this sector. Consequently, total male and female enrolments in universities and girls' colleges had increased from 165,000 in 1995 to more than 263,000 by 1999. This sample period indicates an average annual growth rate of graduates of 16.8 per cent.

During this period a number of community and private colleges, university colleges and research centres were opened. King Khalid University, a consolidation of King Saud University branch and Imam Mohammed bin Saud Islamic university branch in Abha, was established in the Southern Region. About two-

thirds of secondary school graduates entered university during this period. About two-thirds of those entering university were studying humanities rather than sciences which led to an imbalance at graduation of the arts-educated over the science-educated. This caused a problem for the labour market which continued to need more graduates with a scientific background: in the next development period an attempt has been made to redress this imbalance. Emphasis would also be placed on encouraging fields of study which prepare students for the requirements of the labour market.

The private sector was urged to provide practical training for students in the existing private educational establishments and to establish more private colleges. The voluntary field is seen as likely to receive greater participation from students if they were made more aware of the importance of voluntary service and trained in practical ways that could be useful to those wishing to serve in this sector.

The eight universities are: King Saud, King

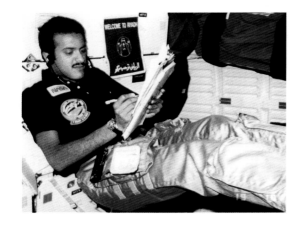

Above:

A highlight of Saudi involvement in science and technology came when, in June 1985, Prince Sultan ibn Salman bin Abdul Aziz Al Saud became the first Saudi Arabian astronaut, and indeed the first Arab, the first Muslim and the first member of royalty in space. The Prince conducted a number of experiments on board NASA's space shuttle Discovery, which advanced international understanding of rocket exhaust gases and the effects of weightlessness on the human body.

Left:

A student engrossed in his studies at King Saud University.

Abdul Aziz, King Faisal, King Fahd UPM, Islamic, Imam, Umm al-Qura and King Khalid. All have separate sections for men and women except for King Fahd University and Islamic University which are for men only.

In mid decade of the new century, the total number of new entrants to the eight universities stood at 203,000 males and 86,000 females. In addition, 200,000 girls were entering girls' colleges, making the total numbers in tertiary education again higher for girls than boys.

Technical Education

"Technical education and vocational training play a fundamental role in the development of Saudi manpower and improving productivity", according to the Seventh Development Plan covering the opening five years of the new century. SR 6.1 billion was allocated to this sector in the Development Plan. There were increases in the enrolment of students in technical secondary education (which stood at 40,000 at the dawn of the century) and in the 35 technical institutes (21,000 in 1999). Other technical institutes under the direct supervision of relevant agencies (Ministry of Health Institutes, Teacher Training Colleges, Ministry of Posts and Telecommunications Institutes, Physical Education Colleges and the two colleges of Jubail and Yanbu) saw increased enrolments, rising from 41,200 in 1998. There are 30 vocational training centres run by GOTEVT, with about 12,300 trainees enrolled at the turn of the century. The Institute of Public Administration (IPA) increased their enrolments in both pre-service and in-service training programmes for government employees. Training programmes in both the private sector and other government agencies also increased. In all of these institutions the Government sought increased participation, efficiency and improved teaching. The drop-out rate has been high in technical education which is wasteful: the reasons behind this were to be researched and efficiency improved. The Government wants to introduce a system for assessing and accrediting the skills required for many occupations.

Research: Science and Technology

The King Abdul Aziz City for Science and Technology (KACST) has long had the function to support research projects in scientific fields, to send students abroad on scholarships, to sponsor trainees inside the Kingdom, to publish a science journal and to add new scientific terms to its data bank. In the next phase of its anticipated development period the private sector will play an enhanced role in establishing Research and Development centres and financially support research at them and the centres already operating. Central to policy for later in the decade 2000-10 is to keep abreast of developments in all aspects of science and technology and information technology and to establish a national base capable of innovating as well as adapting new technology. In information technology at present most products are imported. In the next development period it is expected that, with private sector involvement, information services throughout the Kingdom will be improved and updated and an integrated national service will be set up to which all will be encouraged to have access. The Arabic language will be introduced into the service.

Health

One of the greatest benefits flowing from Saudi Arabia's late twentieth century wealth is the enormously improved system of healthcare which has been made possible. King Faisal decided that the State should provide free medical treatment for all its citizens, and for pilgrims taken ill when visiting the Holy Places of Islam. He initiated a programme of hospital building with the result that there are now no fewer than 350 hospitals in the Kingdom with some 50,000 beds. For some years there have been some 32,000 doctors, 68,000 nurses and 40,000 assistant health personnel working in the Kingdom. Many of these are foreign nationals, who will be supplemented and eventually succeeded by Saudis.

Medical training institutes have been established at Abha and Madinah, and at the

King Abdul Aziz, King Faisal and King Saud Universities. Primary healthcare is covered by 3,500 healthcare centres around the Kingdom and 500 more are planned. All members of society are treated at these centres and then, if necessary, are referred to specialist hospitals. The mobile emergency centres are to be increased, with 130 planned for operation annually during the *hajj* seasons at Makkah and Madinah and on the *hajj* roads. The healthcare provided by Saudi Arabia today is superior to any other in the developing world. The network of health services has been consistently updated to take advantage of the latest advances in medical technology.

Hospitals

There are currently 2.4 hospital beds for every 1,000 citizens, 19 per cent of which are provided by the private sector. Riyadh, with 11 general hospitals, is the best provided city in the Kingdom and has become the centre for most specialized healthcare. The King Faisal Specialist Hospital in Riyadh has attracted specialists of a very high calibre from around the world, including Sweden and Britain: it acts as a referral hospital for cases requiring specialist treatment. It has an impressive ambulance service for those who cannot easily reach the hospital, including air ambulances which land at the hospital's own heliport. Portable cardiac machines and on-board computers in the ambulances and aircraft can relay signals to the main hospital.

Riyadh's King Khalid Eye Specialist Hospital has established a reputation throughout the region as a leader in its field. The hospital can accommodate 260 inpatients and is equipped with 12 operating theatres and two emergency service surgical treatment rooms; two mobile laser coagulators can be used in any one of these facilities. The eye hospital also offers research, diagnosis and treatment services in its several clinics which include optometry, ultra-sonography, radiology, psychophysical and electro-physiology laboratories, as well as a pharmacy and screening center. It has become a leader in the treatment of trachoma, attracting patients from many other countries: the incidence of trachoma in the general population of the Kingdom has decreased significantly. The hospital has also been selected by the World Health Organisation as the centre for combating blindness in the region. Blindness has sharply reduced in recent years. In addition to these specialist hospitals Riyadh has maternity and fever hospitals.

The King Fahd Medical Centre in Yanbu has 342 beds and specialises particularly in burns, ear-nose-and-throat problems, opthalmic surgery and renal dialysis. Designed to meet the needs of both the industrial city and the region, the Medical Centre provides general medical, occupational and environmental health services. There are departments for preventive medicine, environmental and occupational health. Jeddah is provided with five public hospitals, including the King Abdul Aziz General Hospital which can accommodate 440 patients. In addition to these, there are a maternity and paediatrics hospital, an eye hospital, and a specialist chest hospital.

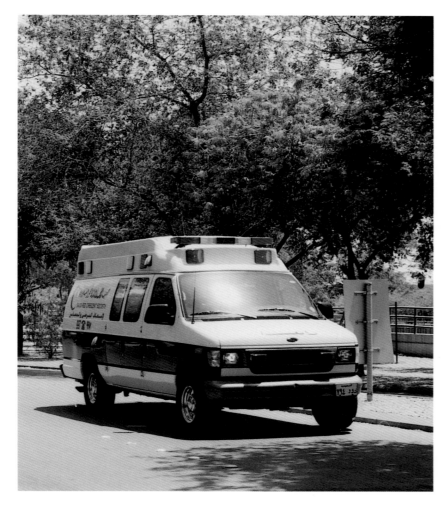

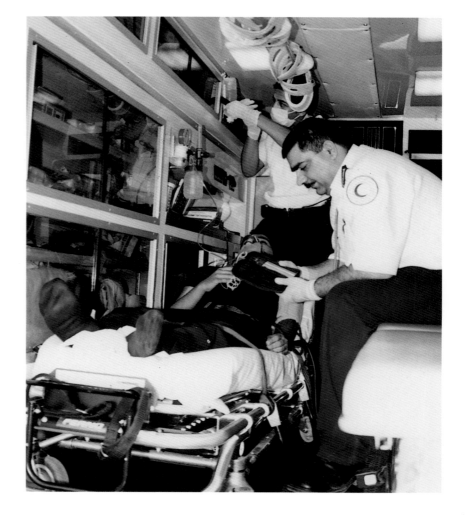

The emergency healthcare infrastructure illustrated opposite has expanded significantly since the 1990s. It is complimented by a network of first-rate private hospitals such as the King Khalid Eye Hospital in Riyadh (above), a leader in its field.

The Holy City of Makkah has been provided with five hospitals to cater for its own and the pilgrims' needs. There are a further 13 hospitals in the Madinah area. Ta'if has three hospitals. The populous Asir in the southwest is provided with seven hospitals spread throughout the region. The Northern Province has four. Qasim has a total of eight hospitals. The populations of the conurbation in the Eastern Province are served by eleven hospitals. The Armed Forces Medical Services and a few other hospitals serving in the remoter areas of the Kingdom also maintain air ambulances and hospital aircraft. The original fleet of mini-hospitals was increased to ten in 1986 when Saudi Arabia took delivery of three L-100-30H5 planes.

The security and military agencies provide healthcare for their staff and families, in their health centres and hospitals. In Riyadh, the Armed Forces Hospital's Cardiology Unit has an international reputation. The King Fahd National Guard Hospital in Riyadh provides medical services for members of the National Guard and their families and also provides care for non-Guard members requiring specialist

treatment, for example heart and liver transplants. It has 550 beds. The National Guard has other hospitals: the King Abdul Aziz National Guard Hospitals in Dammam and al Hasa and the King Khaled National Guard Hospital in Jeddah, with 500 beds. This last offers diagnostic, therapeutic, rehabilitation and emergency services to its members and their families and some services to non-members. In addition to these hospitals, the National Guard opened in 2001 the National Guard King Abdul Aziz Medical City in Riyadh with its eight divisions offering treatments which include cardiac, intensive care and burns, emergency care and trauma, anti-venom and vaccine production and dental services.

The private sector provides health services including hospitals, dispensaries, laboratories, pharmacies and physiotherapy centres. The Saudi Red Crescent Society, which functions much like the Red Cross in Europe, is an important part of the country's system of medical care. It provides first-aid and emergency services, particularly on the roads and during the period of the *hajj*. From a

General Centre in Riyadh, the Society operates three branch offices, eight health centres, 27 first-aid centres which are open 24 hours a day, and 120 ambulances. Ambulances in the *hajj* areas are equipped with radios, and a First-Aid Training Institute has been established. The annual *hajj* confronts the Kingdom with unique health challenges. Pilgrims from Africa, say, or Asia could so easily enter bringing with them communicable diseases like cholera. Special medical teams are briefed for such emergencies. Moreover, the main port of entry, Jeddah, is provided with a quarantine centre containing two isolation hospitals in an enormous site comprising a self-contained village of over 150 buildings.

Preventative Medicine

Research is conducted at many of the larger hospitals, such as the King Faisal Specialist Hospital and at the universities, into the causes and cures of disease. Saudi Arabia is,

climatically, a healthy country. The arid atmosphere, the traditional hardihood of a desert people, sensible dietary customs and the rules of hygiene strictly observed by all good Muslims, combine to prevent the spread of sickness. There is, for example, one of the lowest rates of heart disease per capita in the world. This is particularly true among those living the Bedouin life. There has recently been a great advance in the control and prevention of infectious and endemic diseases, especially diphtheria, whooping cough, measles and the almost total elimination of poliomyelitis. The rates of affliction of bilharzia, malaria and leishmaniasis have declined as research has continued to find cures. The trachoma virus, which attacks the eyes, is a common scourge in hot dry climates, but its incidence has been greatly reduced. There is no settled community in Saudi Arabia beyond the reach of the network of medical care now provided. The urban areas are served by major general and specialist hospitals: elsewhere there are district dispensaries and primary health centres, and even the smallest and most remote desert

Above:

The Kingdom Hospital is a key facility in an extensive new urban development, the Kingdom Compound, to the north of Riyadh, comprising also schools and housing.

Right:

A number of schools for the disabled now exist in Saudi Arabia, such as that in Riyadh. The Disabled Children's Association, a charity under the patronage of HRH Prince Sultan ibn Salman, plays an active role in raising awareness of the needs of disabled children and in organising related research conference.

community has access to mobile clinics and dispensaries, the "flying doctor" and other emergency services. At the same time, there is a continuous programme of vaccination, nutritional instruction, pre- and post-natal care for mothers, x-rays and dental care. Sources of carrier-bred disease, such as malaria and bilharzia, are systematically treated. Infant mortality, once as high as 20 per cent in some desert communities, has fallen sharply, while life expectancy has risen. Health education is itself a form of preventive medicine, and widespread efforts are being made to increase the public's awareness of health problems, their causes and how best to deal with them.

The Handicapped

The Saudi Government, in accordance with the principles of Islam, makes special provision for the care of handicapped people. A school for the blind was established as early as 1959. Since then institutes for the blind and for the deaf-mute

(one for girls and one for boys) have been set up in Riyadh.

There are many other centres for the rehabilitation of the handicapped and for care of the elderly run by the Government. Jeddah has its Institute for Speech and Hearing. Workshops, such as those at the Dammam Institute, train pupils in carpentry, tailoring, secretarial skills, painting, agriculture, horticulture, telephone operating and computer programming. Planning policies for these and future institutions have evolved in the light of experience. In the institutes for the blind, two courses – one academic, the other vocational – are normally provided. Pupils are admitted to the academic courses from the age of six to the age of eighteen, when they can sit the examination for a Secondary Education Certificate. Teaching methods are not dissimilar from those of ordinary schools, except for the use of Braille. For pupils between the ages of six and twenty, vocational training courses are available in such subjects as basketry, weaving and the

manufacture of household equipment. These courses usually extend over six years, and culminate in the examination for a certificate in technology. Some general education is included as well and all pupils are trained to read and write Braille. Amply equipped workshops are available. The items which the pupils can make – chairs, beds, baskets, cane tables, brushes, cloth, carpets – are usually of good quality, and sell quite readily on the open market.

The institutes for the deaf and dumb have to cope with even more difficult problems. A preparatory course is provided for young children aged four to six. Deaf and dumb pupils are fed and clothed, as well as receiving their monthly grant and enjoying the medical and welfare services available to all handicapped people. They are taught in classes containing not more than ten, or fewer than five, pupils. Every institute has social workers and a full-time nurse on the staff. The hope is that all students will acquire a trade, with the encouragement of the Labour Law's stipulations that companies

employing more than 50 should give two per cent of their jobs to disabled workers. In 1985 a General Directorate for Women's and Children's Affairs was set up under the terms of the Fourth Plan with specific provision to provide a section devoted to following up the education of the Kingdom's disabled, and thereafter with monitoring their employment. Those children who are in care have long been encouraged to participate in the Kingdom's everyday life through a full range of extracurricular activities; a policy which has seen the flowering of many an active and fully socially adapted adult.

Voluntary Services and Charities

The Saudi people are very aware of their Islamic duty to care for the less fortunate in their society and the Government has always acknowledged and encouraged the part played by the voluntary services in fund-raising and helping the needy, especially widows, orphans, the elderly and the handicapped. There are some 200 charitable societies in existence with over 27,000 members, providing, amongst other things, schools and day centres for handicapped children and the elderly.

One of the best known of these charitable organisations is the al-Nahda Philanthropic Centre for Women in Riyadh. Al-Nahda was founded by Princess Sarah bint Faisal in 1962, for the "enhancement and development of womens' abilities". Its Rehabilitation Centre runs training programmes for women with particular needs, training them in skills which suit their abilities, for example embroidery, sewing, ceramics and pottery. Its Down Syndrome School helps children with this condition by devising individual educational plans for each child and helping the parents to cope with the condition. Its Social Service Centre caters for the needy by providing housing, making monthly payments to divorcees and orphans, guiding families in trouble and handing out food during Ramadan. Al-Nahda is supported largely by fund-raising activities, in particular its huge and popular annual bazaar.

Above, left to right:

Successive governments have invested heavily to support the welfare needs of the growing population – unemployment benefit, pensions and disability allowances are all part of a safety net administrated by the General Organisation for Social Insurance. Social security covering such a wide and sparse geographical remit, with such a diverse population (some of the range shown above) is ever a challenge, and, with a burgeoning population, one that can only grow over time.

Also in Riyadh, the King Faisal Foundation exists "to improve life for the less fortunate" with educational support to schools and colleges, with scholarships and with philanthropic support, usually in the form of one-off payments, to projects such as the building of a school or clinic. These high-profile projects are run by private initiative and funding. The Foundation funds an annual prize, "the King Faisal International Prize", to acknowledge contributions to research, particularly in the fields of medicine and science which have made a positive difference. The prize has earned international renown and prestige. No fewer than nine winners have gone on to win Nobel prizes.

Social Security and Insurance

No developing country has exceeded Saudi Arabia in its concern for its workers and their families. The Social Security section of the Ministry of Labour and Social Affairs provides assistance to Saudi citizens who are unemployed, widowed, orphaned or disabled, to women living alone, to the families of those serving custodial sentences and to victims of natural disasters. Social Insurance is based on Islamic principles through which the State ensures the worker's safety and provides for a stable future. The General Organization for Social Insurance (GOSI) administers the national insurance scheme, pays allowances and makes payments for compensation to individuals and families. It pays a monthly annuity to the insured employee for the rest of his life, on retirement at 60. Compensation is paid for periods of unemployment and disability payments are made where accidents prevent a man from working. This scheme relies on contributions from employers and employees as well as investment revenues and Government subsidy.

Social Life

Sport

The traditional sports of the Arabian peninsula belong, as might be expected, to the desert and to the nomadic people who inhabit the desert: hawking or falconry, the hunting of game with saluki hounds, and the racing of camels and Arabian horses. Over-hunting in the past drastically reduced the number of game birds and animals. A programme of breeding in captivity and releasing into the wild the most endangered wild animals and birds, the *houbara* bustard, oryx, ibex and gazelles (*see* Chapter 1) has made a start in restoring these creatures to the wild. They are now mainly to be found in and near the areas where they were released, the Protected Areas where hunting is not allowed. Indeed, in 1977 King Khalid banned the use of guns altogether in the interests of conservation. Today coursing of hares and shooting of small birds remain as the only forms of hunting that are still permitted.

Horse racing on the other hand is vigorously promoted and popularly supported. The events at Riyadh's race course are always well attended, with the pleasure of the crowd lying in the speed of the horses and the horsemanship of the jockeys, and not in betting which is contrary to the precepts of Islam. Camel races, which occur frequently in towns and communities in the desert, are held on a yearly basis in Riyadh, at the time of winter's Janadriyah Festival, with the camels carrying their owners' colours.

In 1964 the Saudi Arabian Olympic Committee was formed and in 1984 the Kingdom competed in the Olympic Games for the first time, in football and rifle-shooting. Other fields in which Saudi athletes have distinguished themselves in subsequent years include athletics, cycling, handball, table-tennis, football and volleyball.

The Saudis' greatest achievements, however, have been in the field of football. In 1984 and 1988 the Saudi National Football Team won the Asian Games Gold Cup. In 1989 the Kingdom hosted the fifth World Youth Soccer Cup Championship and was awarded a special commendation for its organisational competence: the Saudi soccer team went on to win the competition. The Saudi soccer team qualified for the World Cup finals in 1994, 1998, 2002 and 2006 and they acquitted themselves well playing against international teams of the highest calibre. In Riyadh the King Fahd International Stadium, inaugurated in March 1988 and built at a cost of SR1.5 billion, has a capacity of 67,000 spectators and contains running tracks, designed to meet the Olympic standard, set around a football pitch. The General Presidency for Youth Welfare has a particular remit to encourage young athletes to compete at international level: to this end it has constructed sports clubs to train budding young athletes all over the country with stadia, swimming pools and all the amenities of modern sports clubs. Students of outstanding merit are singled out for training in their chosen field of sport.

There is widespread enthusiasm for sport among the male population of the country, despite the sometimes crippling heat of summer and shortage of grass. The provision of air-conditioned indoor facilities compensates for this. Women are less well-provided for as sport must be conducted on a segregated basis, but increasingly private gymnasia and swimming-pools cater for the needs of women to exercise. Desert golf-courses have existed for some years on the outskirts of major cities: now grass courses are being added to these facilities. On the Red Sea coast scuba diving has great appeal, especially to the expatriate community, as the reef there is relatively unpolluted. There are plenty of private clubs in compounds and attached to hotels offering gymnasia and swimming pools.

*Football and athletics have long been a focus for professional sports. Here (**opposite**) Saudi Arabia's Mesfer al-Qahtani vies for the ball with Algeria's Bon Azzah Fahem at the Islamic Solidarity Games in Jeddah, 2003. Mohammed Daak (**below right**) distinguishes himself at the World Youth Championships in Morocco in 2005.*

*For several years, there has been an increase in public events taking place in the capital's streets, particularly since the turn of the century. These include the annual Riyadh cycle race (**right**) and annual marathon (**below**).*

The Setting For Life Today
Architecture of the Capital

One of the most exciting aspects of modern Saudi Arabia is the relatively recent appearance in its largest cities of spectacular and innovative examples of modern architecture. Experimentation and innovation has been made possible by the enthusiasm of Saudi sponsors, their generous budgets and the fact that the architects were to some extent working on a blank canvas. Using a light-weight material, airy structures resembling the desert tent were placed over the new Hajj Terminal at Jeddah airport (see page 156), the football stadium in Riyadh and the Tuwaiq Palace in the Diplomatic Quarter, in Riyadh. On a hot day these structures, seen from afar, seem to float like sails and certainly give a feeling of cool spaciousness. Some of the most successful new buildings have incorporated traditional Islamic styles: simple white-domed mosques in Riyadh (the King Abdul Aziz Mosque) and on the Corniche at Jeddah; the nicely reconstructed central square of Riyadh, with its new Grand Mosque; the castle-like Ministry of Foreign Affairs are just a few examples of this. Striking new buildings – the space-ship-like Ministry of the Interior, for example, and the elegantly tapered Faisaliyya and the Kingdom Tower in the distance, two of the tallest buildings in the Middle East – raise Riyadh's profile in all senses and leave a strong impression on the viewer.

*Shown here (**clockwise from top**), the International Stadium in Riyadh; the archway over the main road into Riyadh from the airport, commemorating the centenary of the initiation of the Saudi state; one of the modern office blocks in central Riyadh; and part of the Riyadh skyscape, dominated by three landmark structures: (**from left to right**) the Ministry of the Interior, the Faisaliyya Tower, the Kingdom Tower.*

Way of life

All over Saudi Arabia today traditional patterns of life are being affected both in their outward form and more intimately by swiftly rising levels of education, the dramatic impact of increased income, and the consequences of industrial-isation. Satellite and terrestrial television, the internet, and the surge towards literacy are swiftly expanding the knowledge both of those living in cities and towns and of the peasantry and villagers. The cities have attracted from the outlying areas people whose way of life in the desert had scarcely changed for centuries.

An industrial revolution which, in Europe, gathered pace over generations, has been compressed in Saudi Arabia into a matter of decades. The strains within Saudi Arabian society today are recognised as inevitable. To exploit these strains by occasional acts of coldly calculated armed violence has been the evident intention of extreme reactionaries, as in an assault on the Grand Mosque in Makkah in 1979, and the more recent attack on expatriate compounds in Riyadh (May 12, 2003).

Most Saudis are devout Muslims, yet do not think this to be inconsistent with their country playing their part on the world stage. They are aware of the responsibility they have inherited as guardians of the Holy Shrines of Islam, and feel the need to maintain standards on behalf of Islam. The central factor in Saudi Arabia's social life is the strength of the family. In a period of swift outward change, widely spread family links produce a complex of allegiances. The Qur'anic prohibition against alcohol is taken seriously. Modesty is expected of women and the segregation of the sexes in open society is widely accepted, despite its being modified in certain aspects. If such a role has meant restrictions on the lives of women, it has nonetheless brought strength to the family unit. In the streets women go veiled; in their homes, with their families or other women and in segregated gatherings outside the home, women-only shops, schools and universities, they are unveiled. Women may not drive; yet now as educated as men, they attend their own secondary schools and colleges, and mixed universities where they

are mainly taught by women. Occasional lectures given by male professors are given by closed circuit television. Saudi women now carry their own passports, their unveiled faces appearing in the photographs. They are entering the work-force in increasing numbers and fields of work.

Marriages arranged between families are still popular, with the girl's parents negotiating the match and the dowry. However, an element of choice by the young people themselves is creeping in, especially among those girls who are becoming wage earners and therefore have more influence in their families, and among those who travel and study abroad. Tradition is still strong, however, and most modern love-matches will not be made without the parents' consent. Qur'anic law provides quite clearly for marriages which do not work. Divorces take place privately, without fuss. Love of privacy is a strong factor in Saudi Arabian life. As elsewhere in the Islamic world, homes are built around an open centre. They do not look outwards: they are self-contained.

The majority of Saudi Arabia's population today live in urban centres in a cosmopolitan city atmosphere (such as the suburb of Riyadh shown **opposite**) – a lifestyle very different from that of their parents a generation ago. While the setting may sometimes have changed, the values are still being handed down largely unaltered. The children in the playground of a Riyadh school (**above**) will study a curriculum centred around Qur'anic teachings. The youths seated in the café whose decor could place it anywhere in the world (**right**) will continue to wear the thobe *as a mark of national identity. The emerging Saudi Arabia will be a complex mixture of tradition and international modernity.*

231

The Bedouin Way of Life

Beyond the towns and cities, among the Bedouin, it is the tribal allegiances that still strongly prevail. The influence of the ancient, disciplined and dignified way of life markedly pervades all levels of Saudi Arabian society. Even in the cities, although the force of tribal loyalties is certainly diminished, it is not forgotten. Among those from the families who hold the leadership of tribes and who have come to live in cities and make their fortunes, there prevails a widespread tendency to maintain the tribal links. The Bedouin "wing" of the family or tribe is visited at festival times throughout the year. In the desert, the social life of the Bedouin, – literally "the desert people" – retains much of its time-honoured forms and styles. Life is centred on the family tent. The traditional black tent is woven by the women of goat hair (the most waterproof), sometimes mixed with sheep's wool and camel hair, in strips which are sewn together. Gaily coloured woven internal "walls" divide the men's section from the general living quarters where the women do the cooking and the small children's leather cradles are slung between tent poles. Many of the desert artefacts are of camel leather or goat hide – belts and waterskins, bags (often decorated with beads and shells) and saddles and cradles and, in the past, shields.

The well-ordered tented home is the responsibility of the women while the camels, herds of goats and milking, are the men's responsibility. Pick-up trucks have supplemented, but not supplanted, the camel, just as bore holes and pumps have supplemented wells. The camel is irreplaceable in true desert travel, which the Bedouin's search for grazing requires. An Arabian camel can survive in winter, when there is moisture in the pasturage, for about a week without being watered, although in high summer only for two or three days. She-camels are the most useful. They produce milk for up to six months after giving birth, and they possess greater stamina than the male. It is the she-camel that is used for riding by mankind; the male camel carries the baggage. White camels are widely admired in Arabia, although in the past the darker-hued well-camouflaged camel was sometimes preferred in the activity of raiding, in which the tribes were often engaged. By night, camels are often hobbled to keep them close to the tent, though the family herds (of an average number of 40 or 50 beasts) always preserve the homing instinct. The branding mark, or *wasm*, distinguishes tribal or clan ownership.

Desert hospitality is invariably generous and leisurely, and attendance upon the guests a distinct obligation. The visitor is welcomed by a rug spread on the ground. He will first be offered tea, and in due course the ceremony of coffee will begin. A few coffee

*The modern ceremonies of offering coffee to guests (**opposite, left**) hark from a tradition that goes back to desert life, as does the* majlis *seating arrangement which is unchanged in an urban or desert tent dwelling (**opposite, right**). Today, picnics in the desert (**above**) are a purely recreational activity, a chance for city-dwellers to celebrate the desert that lies beyond their urban confines.*

beans are roasted on an iron skillet, then placed in a decorated pot to cool. Three times the coffee is brought to the boil, then poured into the characteristic sharp-snouted coffee pot containing ground cardamom seeds, from which it is served in tiny handleless cups. Then, if the visitor is to stay, and is of significance, a young goat or sheep will be slaughtered, roasted, and served up on a great heap of steaming rice.

The Bedouin way of life is hard, uncluttered and unhurried; it brings a closeness to God to those who live it fully. Tribesmen visiting cities or towns unfailingly find hospitality at the homes of relatives or tribal leaders who now reside in the urban communities. The Western visitor is frequently struck by the way in which drivers or servants may be ushered into the presence of the mighty along with distinguished visitors. This accords with the tradition which still to some extent continues which gives every person,

however humble, the right to visit the *majlis*, or open session, of his tribal chief, the sheikh or even the Monarch, with requests for help or intervention in a dispute. All are equal in the sight of God; bowing and scraping do not take place in the Saudi court or society. In the desert, the life of the women is relatively less sequestered than in the cities. Veiling is largely unnecessary. There are no strangers in the group. Worship takes place within the group. In the Bedouin encampment, there is no mosque – where the male presence is predominant – to separate the sexes. Tasks of every kind must be performed jointly.

Despite the onslaught of technology, Saudis as a whole assuredly esteem their old traditional way of life and many city dwellers seeking a break from the hurly-burly of modern life return to spend days and nights in the desert, to enjoy again for a short while the simple life of their forefathers.

Population and the Labour Market

Population counts made in the first half-decade of the 21st century put the total population at about 20.8 million, with only 74.8 per cent of this figure representing Saudis. Significantly, over 60 per cent of the population is under 20 years old. As with other fast developing countries, there has been considerable movement of people from the land to the towns. Even with this influx, large numbers of foreign workers have been needed to supplement the indigenous work-force. Most come for a period and then return home. At the turn of the century, Britain, for example, had about 30,000 nationals working in the Kingdom and the USA a similar number – figures which had not significantly diminished by the middle of the decade. Large contingents have come from such Arab states as Egypt, Jordan, Sudan, Yemen, Palestine, and also from Pakistan. Lebanon and Syria have also provided temporary additions to the population. South Korea, Taiwan and the Philippines have provided manpower and technical skills: Western countries have for the most part provided expertise.

A central concern of the Government's most recent development plan is the reduction of the Kingdom's dependence on this foreign workforce. Saudis nationals, on the whole, have been more attracted to work in the public than the private sector. They have lacked the skills needed for work in the industrial, commercial and professional sectors, where many jobs have been taken by non-Saudis. To alter this imbalance, the Government has resolved to initiate new training and education programmes for Saudis and to ensure that education is directed to preparing graduates of schools, universities and Technical Colleges for the requirements of the labour market.

A huge increase in the numbers of Saudi graduates of schools, universities and technical colleges were expected to come onto the market early in the second decade of

The way of life is evolving rapidly. Traditional suqs (like that of Riyadh **above**) and feasts (**right**) are among the many features that provide continuity, while family life illustrated **opposite** is still the mainstay of the social fabric. Crucial in society's evolution, however, are a change in attitudes to work – a move away from the usually less demanding public sector jobs to the private sector, harnessing the Kingdom's increasingly better-educated workforce to build a vibrant and diverse economy.°

*Rural communities still carefully shelter their womenfolk from the outside world. These girls from the Asir region (**above**) would be unlikely to travel widely. Life for girls in the major cities (**opposite**) can be very different, with new communication technologies, such as the mobile phone and internet, broadening horizons and expectations.*

the century; thereafter, if they have the right qualifications to meet the needs of the developing labour market, it might be seen as desirable to confine certain jobs to Saudis.

Investment in small businesses by the Saudi Credit Bank is today encouraged. Services providing information or manpower were in prospect, for employers and potential employees became aware of each others' needs.

The Government is also pledged to promote more opportunities for women, within *shar'iah* law. Traditionally the only opportunities open to women have been in education and health, but recently women have been encouraged to make use of their education and training and to take up work in many other fields. There are now women working in civil service roles as mathematicians, scientists, teachers, professors, administrators, nurses, doctors, media personnel and social workers. In the private sector women are working in agriculture, banking, trade, real estate, interior design, pharmacology, biology and biochemistry.

Saudi women have always been active in business: indeed the Prophet's wife, Khadija, was a prominent business woman in her own right. A 2004 survey showed that Saudi women have a 34 per cent stake in private businesses in Riyadh and 25.6 per cent in Jeddah. There are estimated to be 5,000 business women in Riyadh and 4,000 in Jeddah. Nationally Saudi women hold 20 per cent of corporate shares, 15 per cent of private companies and 10 per cent of the country's property. They hold nearly 70 per cent of all bank accounts in the Kingdom with deposits worth SR 62 billion. It is now recognised that women represent a huge potential addition to the Saudi work force. King Abdullah said recently, "When we talk about the comprehensive development that our country is witnessing, we cannot ignore the role of Saudi women and their participation in this development". As long as jobs can be provided for them within the constraints of Islamic mores, more opportunities must and will be made available to them.

Glossary

abal	scarlet-fruited shrub, eglantine
adabi	arts stream at secondary school
afri	Saudi gazelle
AH	'*anno hijirae*' i.e. the year, as numbered, according to the Islamic lunar calendar, dating from the *Hijrah* (see below) of the Prophet in AD 622
amir at-tarab	'prince of enchantment', lute
ardah	men's traditional sword dance
arfaj	yellow-flowered shrub
Ayam al Arab	'The Days of the Arabs'
Bai'ah	consultative process
bayt Allah	House of God
birkat	reservoir
boum	boat
dahl	cave
dallah	coffee pot
dhub	plant-eating lizard
Dhu 'l Hijjah,	the twelfth month in the Islamic calendar (in which the *hajj* occurs)
Fatwa	judicial opinions
Futuhat Makkiyah	('Makan Illumination'), by Spanish Muslim mystic, Ibn Arabi
ghaf	tree of acacia family
ghutrah	headcloth worn by Arab men
hadh	prickly saltbush
Hadith	traditions giving the sayings or acts of the Prophet
Hajar al-Aswad,	the Black Stone in the Ka'abah
hajj	pilgrimage to Makkah and other holy places obligatory for every Muslim
hajji	Muslim who has performed the *hajj*
hara	quarter of a city
harrah	extensive lava fields
Haram	the Holy Ka'abah Sanctuary
Haramayn	the two holy cities of Makkah and Madinah
Hijrah	the migration of the Prophet from Makkah to Madinah in AD 622, the year from which the Islamic calendar dates
hijrah	encampment; agricultural settlement
hima	set-aside land
houbara	MacQueen's bustard
idmi	mountain gazelle
ihram	pilgrim's dress
ijtihad	fresh thinking
Ikhwan	'the Brethren', specifically a religious movement founded by King Abdul Aziz
ilmi	scientific stream at secondary school
jamrah	pillar
jar Allah	God's neighbour
Ka'abah	venerated square stone building in the Great Mosque, Makkah, which all Muslims face when praying
Kiswah	black cloth covering the Ka'abah
mahkhara	incense holder
majlis	session for meetings and audiences
maksar	camel saddle litter
Markab	'the ship', tribal standard
mas'a	running place between al-Safa and al-Marwah
masjid	mosque
Al-Masjid al-Haram	Sacred Mosque, Makkah

mashrabiyya	lattice window in the Egyptian style
Mataf	sacred pilgrimage area around the Ka'abah
Mihrab	prayer niche in a mosque indicating the direction of the Ka'abah, cf *qibla*
mubarrad	wooden tray
Muharram	month in the Islamic calendar
Mutawwa	religious police charged with upholding Islamic orthodoxy
Mutawwif	guide for pilgrims performing the *Hajj*
oud	lute
Qasidah	ode
qasr	castle or fort
qibla	wall recess in a mosque indicating the direction of the Ka'abah in Makkah
Qiran	combined performance of the *Hajj* and *Umrah*
rababa	simple violin
Rajajil	'the men' (the standing stones)
Ramadan	ninth month of the Islamic year, a time of fasting
rajaz	song with lines of four or six beats
ratel	honey badger
reem	sand gazelle
rimth	saltbush
Sa'y	the running from as-Safa to al-Marwa in the *Hajj*
sabkhah	salt basins
sayyid	descendant of the Prophet
Shahadatayn	confession, declaration of faith
Shari'ah	Islamic law derived from the Qur'an
sharif	the Prophet's descendants and their families, a wider meaning than *sayyid*
shura	'consultation'
Sura	chapter of the Qur'an
siq	narrow gorge or cannon forming passageway through rock
suq	space in town where the market is held
sukuti sunnah	(tacit) sunnah
Sunnah	the 'way' of the Prophet; orthodox interpretation and commentary on the life of the Prophet and the Qur'an
Talbiyah	words of acceptance of the pilgrimage duties chanted by the *Hajj* pilgrims
Tamattu	separate performance of *Hajj* and *Umrah*
Tawaf	circumambulation of Ka'abah
tawaf al-wida	farewell *tawaf*
tawjihiyyah	Saudi Baccalaureat, taken at end of secondary education
thobe	inner gown worn by Arab men
Ulema	Muslim scholars; scholars of Islamic law (singular: *alim*)
Umm Salim	'Salim's Mother', hoopoe lark
umrah	short form of pilgrimage to Makkah only
uruq	crescent sand dunes
usht	annual plants
wadi	former water course, now dry
wasm	branding mark
Wudu	ablutions before prayers
Wukuf	final prayer of the *Hajj* made standing on Mount Arafat
yadd al-hamam	mortar
Zakat	regular giving of fixed alms

Index

Names beginning with al- have been entered under the first letter of the following word. We have not distinguished between the 'ayn and the glottal stop, using the closing quotation mark for both sounds. Although an inexact science, attempts have been made to be consistent in the transliteration of Arab words. Pages shown in italics indicate an illustration.